ASYLUM BY BOAT

Dr Claire Higgins is an historian and a senior research associate at the Andrew and Renata Kaldor Centre for International Refugee Law at UNSW. She is a Fulbright Postdoctoral Scholar, and completed doctoral study in History as a Clarendon Scholar at the University of Oxford. Claire has previously held the Margaret George Award at the National Archives of Australia, and in 2017 she held a visiting Postdoctoral Fellowship through the Australia–European University Institute Fellowship Association Inc., to pursue research into safe pathways to protection for asylum seekers.

ASYLUM BY BOAT
ORIGINS OF AUSTRALIA'S REFUGEE POLICY

CLAIRE HIGGINS

UNSW PRESS

A UNSW Press book

Published by
NewSouth Publishing
University of New South Wales Press Ltd
University of New South Wales
Sydney NSW 2052
AUSTRALIA
newsouthpublishing.com

© Claire Higgins 2017
First published 2017

10 9 8 7 6 5 4 3 2 1

Cataloguing-in-Publication entry is available at the National Library of Australia
Creator: Higgins, Claire, author.
Title: Asylum by boat : origins of Australia's refugee policy / Dr Claire Higgins.
ISBN: 9781742235677 (paperback)
      9781742244044 (epub)
      9781742248424 (ePDF)
Notes: Includes index.
Subjects: Boat people–Government policy–Australia.
          Political refugees–Government policy–Australia.
          Refugees–Government policy–Australia–History.
          Australia–Emigration and immigration–Government policy.

Design Josephine Pajor-Markus
Cover design Alissa Dinallo
Cover images Michael Jensen, National Library of Australia; *above:* Customs officer Frank Dalton holding a Vietnamese refugee child, Xye Than Hue, Darwin, November 1977 (PIC/8943/4); *below:* Vietnamese boat people, Darwin, November 1977 (PIC/8943/3).
Printer Griffin Press

UNSW
SYDNEY

Contents

Introduction

On Saturday 3 May 1975, twelve families signed a letter to the Australian government. The men and women introduced themselves as librarians, teachers, police officers and nurses from Vietnam, and with their sixteen children they were sheltered in Singaporean waters, aboard a 24-metre fishing boat. Just days earlier the families had fled Saigon along with thousands of other residents, when advancing North Vietnamese forces attacked the outskirts of the city and Saigon 'fell' on 29 April 1975, marking the end of the United States' war in Vietnam. In the letter the families explained how they had sailed under gunfire from the river bank and out into the open sea 'to save our lives'. 'Some of the fleeing boats', they wrote, 'were hit by the shore fire and burnt but we were probably lucky'.[1] And they added that once they could take aboard provisions, they would sail south in the 'strong belief' that the government and people of Australia 'will accept us with pity in the country as refugees'. Together the families pledged: 'We will do our best for the rest of our lives to contribute to the Commonwealth of the Royal Australia'.

We do not know the fate of these families. Their letter was strategically cited at a news conference, held that Saturday by Singapore's Ministry of Defence to publicise the challenge Singapore was suddenly facing, along with other letters addressed to the United States Embassy and the Singaporean government. These notes had been penned by just a few of the more than 6500 refugees who reached Singapore that week aboard wooden fishing boats, large trawlers and tankers.[2] Many people arrived with nothing. Singaporean welfare societies collected donations of food and clothing, and refugees with shrapnel wounds were taken to hospital.[3] Thousands more Vietnamese refugees had escaped by boat to Thailand or out into open seas, and were reported adrift on barges or fishing boats, hungry and exhausted, desperate for fresh water and a tow to land.[4]

In Canberra, Deputy Secretary of the Department of Prime Minister and Cabinet, Geoffrey Yeend, was paying close attention to news of the arrivals in Singapore harbour. Australia's Labor government, led by Prime Minister Gough Whitlam, was not yet prepared to commit to resettling any of the refugees. On 8 May Yeend advised the Department of Foreign Affairs that in the meantime his 'chief concern' was avoiding 'unfavourable publicity' for the government.[5]

That night the phone rang, and Yeend was told by Kenneth Rogers from Foreign Affairs that Singaporean authorities were helping the Vietnamese refugees to press on, and were handing out navigational charts for Australia and the Philippines.[6] Foreign Affairs sent cables to missions in Geneva, New York and Washington, appealing for the United Nations High Commissioner for Refugees (UNHCR) to pressure Singapore to 'hold the ships' until 'arrangements could be made'.[7] As yet the Australians were not sure what these arrangements might be.

The next morning Yeend gathered with the Deputy Secretary of the Department of Foreign Affairs JR Rowland and Acting Prime Minister Dr Jim Cairns to talk over the idea that if some people did leave Singapore and head south, the navy would need to meet and escort them 'to the appropriate reception points'.[8] Yeend returned to his office to write up his notes. A highly regarded public servant, described as calm and unflappable, Yeend would later head Prime Minister and Cabinet under the Liberal/National Coalition government led by Prime Minister Malcolm Fraser.[9] On this morning, Yeend put into words an idea that would come to occupy successive Australian governments: '[…] if ships were sailing towards Australia we would need to look something better than helpless'.[10]

In using this expression Yeend was referring to the logistics of managing and aiding vulnerable people, as Singaporean authorities and charities were doing at that very moment, but his choice of words also reflected a belief that government must control (and appear to control) entry to Australia. As a white, settler society on the edge of Asia, control of entry was a founding principle at Australia's federation in 1901. It is a 'pillar' of Australian immigration policy, according to leading immigration scholar James Jupp, and the nation's population has been 'planned and engineered to a greater extent than is true for almost anywhere else'.[11]

Australia is a signatory to the 1951 Convention relating to the Status of Refugees and its 1967 Protocol (the Refugee Convention), which are the chief instruments under which states have made commitments to one another 'in good faith' to protect people who are fleeing persecution.[12] Yet the Australian government views the arrival of asylum seekers by boat, without valid visas, as challenging control of entry. Further, these boats attract media interest and public disquiet that is disproportionate to their numbers. Peter Mares has described this as the product of a society that is 'hostile to its foundations' as 'one of the world's true immigrant nations'.[13] In his book, *Borderline: Australia's treatment of refugees and asylum seekers*, Mares drew a parallel between the response to boat arrivals in contemporary Australia and an historic sense of geographic vulnerability within the national psyche:

> There is a deeply held, yet irrational anxiety that
> Australia is perpetually in danger of being overrun;

that our sovereignty is brittle and our borders are weak.
It is as though this continent were a rickety lifeboat,
and all the world's oppressed and poor are desperately
swimming towards us, threatening to drag us under.[14]

By 11 May 1975, many of the refugees in Singapore harbour
had accepted charts, fuel and provisions, and had departed
in the hope of sailing to the United States' territory of
Guam thousands of kilometres to the north-east or, somewhat closer, Subic Bay in the Philippines.[15] At an inter-
departmental meeting a week later, on 19 May 1975, staff
from Labor and Immigration, Foreign Affairs, Prime Minister and Cabinet, and seven other departments worked
through possible courses of action should some of the refugees sail to Australia. They noted that if a boat arrived it
would likely attract media attention, and believed that if
those on board were allowed to land the precedent would
not go unnoticed in countries to Australia's north, whether
in relation to an ongoing exodus of Vietnamese or future
political unrest 'in countries to our immediate north'.[16]

The departments noted the need to consider Australia's
obligations under the Refugee Convention toward asylum
seekers arriving in Australia. They debated whether a boat
could be prevented from entering Australia's territorial
waters in the first place, perhaps re-fuelled and directed
elsewhere, although recognised 'it would be very difficult to
insist on the departure of a boat […] in view of the distance

and difficulty involved in reaching any alternative country of sanctuary'.[17] They then proposed that a boat be allowed to land and passengers taken into custody, and based on the briefing paper they prepared, Prime Minister Whitlam chose the option of custody.[18] But the boats did not arrive on his government's watch.

By the time five young Vietnamese refugees steered their way into Darwin harbour in April 1976, the Fraser government was in office. Just over 2000 more refugees would arrive by boat between 1976 and 1981, during which time more than a million refugees would flee Indochina, and the Fraser government would work through the same issues its predecessor did at that interdepartmental meeting in May 1975. How did the Fraser government attempt to control the maritime arrival of asylum seekers, and to look, in Yeend's words, 'better than helpless'? That process will be the main focus of this book.

There are good reasons to examine these questions. Since 1989, when asylum seekers from South-East Asia arrived by boat once again, successive Australian governments implemented increasingly restrictive legislation and asylum policy. This included the introduction of mandatory detention in 1992 by the Labor government of Prime Minister Paul Keating. The changes that had occurred in immigration policy and political debate in the intervening period are the focus of the final chapter of this book, an attempt to bridge the response to asylum seekers in the two eras, and provide a sense of how policy became increasingly restrictive from that point on. In the early 2000s, after the Howard government introduced policies of extra-territorial detention and intercepting and turning boats around at sea, Matthew J Gibney wrote in his comparative study *The Ethics and Politics of Asylum* that Australia had become 'arguably the most unwelcoming country towards asylum seekers in the Western world'.[19] In 2014, after these practices had been revived under the Gillard and Rudd Labor governments, and militarised under 'Operation Sovereign Borders' by the Liberal/National Abbott government, the UN High Commissioner for Human Rights Zeid Ra'ad Al Hussein described Australian asylum policy as 'leading to a chain of human rights violations'.[20] Today, mandatory detention and 'turn-backs' at sea are cornerstones of the Australian government's asylum policy, and generate controversy for breaches of Australia's obligations under international law and for the alleged abuse of the rights of asylum seekers and refugees.

Former prime minister Fraser used his own record to be a vocal critic of policies under later governments.[21] In doing so he painted a picture of his own government's decision making in which 'a moral and ethical obligation' to accept Vietnamese boat arrivals and to resettle Indochinese refugees overrode public or political opposition, and proposals for detention facilities were dismissed.[22] The picture is consistent with what is known of Fraser's leadership style, described by political scientist Patrick Weller as one in which Fraser would 'adopt a stand and require others to explain why it should not be adopted'.[23]

Sitting in the former prime minister's office on a bright Melbourne morning in December 2010, we discussed the fall of Saigon and its consequences for Australian immigration history. At one point during our conversation, I asked:

'When your government was faced with the Vietnamese refugee situation, what were the choices in front of you?'

'Well, say yes say no.'

'It was as black and white as that?'

'What else could you do?'[24]

Fraser's response may seem simplistic, but it is a question that resides at the heart of contemporary asylum policy debate in Australia (and many other refugee-receiving countries), and it is the reason why the Fraser era holds interest within the Australian media and academy.

Given the hardening of asylum policy in Australia over the past two decades, and similar developments in North America and Europe, there are clearly other answers to Fraser's question. And the evidence presented in this book from Australian government archival records indicates that other answers were floated within and/or by the Department of Immigration and Ethnic Affairs. These included turning the boats back at sea, and the possible detention of asylum seekers and refugees arriving by boat (which was submitted to Cabinet). These measures were not implemented, and were publicly rejected by the Minister for Immigration and the secretary of that department, but their existence on paper reflects the nature of the decision-making process at various levels of government, what Fraser once described as 'the vast co-operative effort of departments and ministers to see that a proposal is fleshed out, examined, options considered and decisions taken'.[25] Of course, the archival records cannot fully reflect how these options were talked over in informal conversations or thought through by departmental staff or members of Cabinet. Where possible I have included excerpts from interviews that I conducted between 2010 and 2012 with Fraser and his former Immigration ministers Michael MacKellar and Ian Macphee, as well as departmental staff, among others. These interviews predated the availability of some of the archival evidence cited in this book, but in other cases their memories, while potentially shaped by their opinion of policy under later governments, offered an important additional perspective on the policy-making context.

Records created by UNHCR provide another side to the story, and offer a unique and valuable perspective on the development of Australia's approach to asylum seekers during these years. In the 1970s and early 1980s, the UN refugee agency had an office in Sydney just up the hill from Circular Quay. Staff liaised with the government of the day over asylum seekers, refugee resettlement and aid for humanitarian relief programs abroad. They held private conversations with Department of Immigration and Ethnic Affairs officials, and at the time were privy to decision making on individual refugee applications – and they took notes. One staff member, the Legal Adviser for UNHCR in Australia, later became the world's leading legal expert on the Refugee Convention and a distinguished professor at the University of Oxford. His name is Professor Guy S Goodwin-Gill. Thoughtfully, Goodwin-Gill donated his notes to one of the libraries at Oxford, and these files inform the analysis throughout this book. They are a particularly important addition to the historical understanding of Australia's response to the Vietnamese boat arrivals, capturing the UN refugee agency's assessment of Australian asylum policy and practice.

Academics and journalists have also engaged with the comparison between then and now, debating whether or how Australia could have responded to asylum seekers in a principled and humane way in this earlier era. Some have argued that the Fraser government exhibited 'exemplary generosity' toward Vietnamese people arriving in Australia by boat.[26] Writing in the *Australian* newspaper in 2010, Mike Steketee described Fraser as displaying 'courageous leadership' in the face of a regional refugee situation far greater in size than those confronted by later governments.[27] Others have argued that the government's response was 'grudging' at best.[28] In the same newspaper in 2015, Greg Sheridan claimed that Fraser was 'the father of offshore processing', because his government had sought to process Vietnamese refugees out of camps in the region before these same people chose to sail to Australia (a vastly different policy from the extra-territorialised system of prolonged detention that recent Australian governments have maintained in Papua New Guinea and Nauru).[29] If we are to better understand Australia's refugee history in the Fraser era, there is a real need for further archival research and nuanced analysis.

The most comprehensive study of the Fraser government's response to the boats and resettlement of Indochinese refugees is Nancy Viviani's *The Long Journey: Vietnamese migration and settlement in Australia*. This book was published in 1984, before a comparison with later governments was possible. Then a senior academic in the field of Asian studies and political science, Viviani also had Foreign Affairs experience. She made the following conclusion:

> The first and most enduring conclusion to be drawn, is that Australian governments have upheld international law and custom on refugees […] It has not only proved of immense humanitarian benefit […] [it] has been an example to other states.[30]

This assessment has been echoed by prominent scholars writing on refugee law or immigration policy more generally, such as Mary Crock, Matthew Gibney and James Jupp, among others.[31] Former Australian diplomat and former Assistant High Commissioner for Protection at UNHCR, Erika Feller, has said Australia was once known as 'a country where international responsibilities were taken seriously and honoured'.[32] This is despite the fact that as the flight of people from Indochina increased dramatically in 1978, Fraser's then Minister for Immigration, Michael MacKellar, and the Department of Immigration and Ethnic Affairs would express a frank view that 'we are locked into international obligations towards refugees [...] [and] Australia's credibility and status as a civilized, compassionate nation are under test'.[33]

Importantly, Viviani both noted the Fraser government's commitment 'to international law and custom' and acknowledged, in a 1985 paper, that Australia's refugee policy is informed by the self-interested desire to offset international criticism and manage asylum flows.[34] The idea that these two objectives can be compatible with Australia's international obligations is reflected in my analysis.

In a book such as this, it is impossible to do justice to the story of Vietnamese, Lao and Cambodian refugees during the 1970s to 1990s, or to the complexities of the international and regional response to their plight. The history has been expertly detailed by W Courtland Robinson, among others, in his 1998 book, *Terms of Refuge: The Indochinese exodus and the international response*. It is important to note here, however, that countries in the region, including Malaysia and Thailand, were hosting vastly greater numbers of displaced Indochinese than Australia ever received, and were as concerned about the reaction within their own communities to these displaced people as Australia was.

The scope of this book is confined to Australia's response to fewer than 3000 asylum seekers arriving by boat from 1976 to the early 1990s. Most (if not all) of those who sailed to Australia between 1976 and 1981 were from Vietnam, and all but one of these boats arrived before 1980, while in the latter period boat arrivals were largely from Cambodia, Vietnam, and the People's Republic of China. The book spans an era in which immigration and refugee policies – and political debate about these policies – were adapting to the move away from more than seventy years of racially discriminatory entry referred to as 'White Australia'. The concept of a White Australia had originated within a sense of racial and labour solidarity between settler nations in the 19th and early 20th centuries, imbued with a special sense of geographic vulnerability on the edge of Asia.

Guided by the imperatives of a White Australia, the 'planning and engineering' of the country's population from the end of the Second World War to the early 1970s had included resettling some 300 000 mostly European refugees.[35] Many were selected for their perceived value to Australia's economic and demographic development. These refugees have since been described as a test case for large-scale non-British immigration to Australia, laying the foundations for a multicultural society.[36] At the time, however, their resettlement was described by the Department of Immigration as 'an ambitious social experiment'.[37]

The Whitlam government took office at the close of this large-scale post-war immigration program, by which time the White Australia Policy had been modified under the *Migration Act 1958* (Cth), and slowly dismantled through to 1973. A desire to improve Australia's reputation within Asia and internationally is widely considered to have contributed to the policy's demise. Meg Gurry and Gwenda Tavan have shown how this process was informed by criticism from the Department of External Affairs (the precursor to Foreign Affairs), which believed that the Department of Immigration did not appreciate the challenges that racially discriminatory entry policy presented for Australian diplomats overseas, particularly in their dealings with newly independent states in South-East Asia, and Tavan has shown how the policy was softened through the efforts of Hubert Opperman as Minister for Immigration in the Liberal government of Prime Minister Harold Holt, and long-serving Immigration department secretary (and former diplomat) Peter Heydon.[38] But although Whitlam declared in

1973 that by moving away from discriminatory immigration policy, Australia would now enjoy 'a growing standing as a distinctive, tolerant, cooperative and well regarded nation', not only in Asia 'but in the world at large', he is commonly remembered as being unwilling to resettle Vietnamese refugees.[39] Whitlam reportedly feared that the Vietnamese who were fleeing the fall of Saigon would be biased against a Labor government; the view was shared by some Labor Party colleagues, informing the party's response to the issue of boat arrivals during the late 1970s.[40]

Under Whitlam both the immigration and refugee intakes were significantly reduced. Alongside his government's concern for changing economic conditions, particularly in the manufacturing sector, the idea of promoting a non-discriminatory policy was to give the 'appearance that immigration had radically changed' while 'running little risk of alienating voters'.[41] A concern for the way that non-white immigration would be received within the Australian community had even been shared by those who argued passionately for non-discriminatory policy, such as the respected Immigration Reform movement, a collection of professionals and academics that Tavan credits with a leading role in advocating for policy change.[42] As the policy was being dismantled through the 1960s, the group held that: 'In deciding on the numbers to be admitted from particular sources, race and colour could be taken into account if public attitudes in Australia made this advisable'.[43]

There was an abiding belief within and outside government that immigration should be sufficiently controlled so as to keep the country 'reasonably free from racial tension'.[44] It is for this reason that the Indochinese who were eventually resettled in Australia are regarded as the first real test of the end of White Australia.[45] During the period I examine in this book, the mid-1970s to mid-1990s, around 150 000 Vietnamese settled in Australia, alongside several thousand Cambodians and Lao who had escaped simultaneous upheaval and repression.[46]

When those twelve families were anchored in Singaporean waters, however, in May 1975, Australia had ratified the 1967 Protocol to the Refugee Convention (which removed temporal and geographic limitations under the latter instrument), but the nation's obligations under international refugee law had not been incorporated into the *Migration Act 1958* and there was no formal procedure for assessing applications for refugee status under the Convention once people stepped ashore.[47] People fleeing persecution had sought refuge in Australia before this, by jumping ship, defecting from diplomatic postings, or crossing into Australian-administered territory, for example, but as historian Klaus Neumann has detailed, successive Australian governments chose myriad ways of responding to these individuals, depending (for example) on where they fled from, the public response to their plight, or how they fitted migration criteria rather than their status as refugees under the Convention.[48] During the first half of the 1970s an American lawyer called Frank A Bauman was the UNHCR's senior officer in Australasia, and in this role he found that because Australia lacked formal procedure for determining refugee claims at that time, it exercised deportation practices that risked sending people back to persecution (a potential breach of the principle of *non-refoulement* set out under Article 33(1) of the Convention).[49]

It would take until 1977 for the government to announce a formal refugee policy and status determination procedure. During this time an inquiry by the Senate Standing Committee on Foreign Affairs and Defence found that whether Australia's previous military involvement in Vietnam was right or wrong, it was seen to have a 'very heavy' moral responsibility to aid those who 'had assisted our forces there and whose lives were believed to be in danger because of this assistance'.[50] In June 1976 the Committee concluded that Australia could not allow the 'unrestricted entry of tens of thousands of refugees', but that the government had to establish a way of responding to this and other urgent humanitarian situations. It recommended the urgent establishment of 'administrative machinery' and policy guidelines for Australia's response to refugees, including an ongoing and identifiable refugee intake, and noted that the admission of refugees and other displaced persons should reflect the 'spirit' of Australia's obligations under the Refugee Convention.[51]

The Coalition had set out the need for a formal response to refugees in its policy platform of August 1975, when it was still in Opposition.[52] Backed by the Senate committee's recommendation, a form of policy was in the pipeline, but the arrival of a handful of refugees by boat through 1976 nudged the issue along. In a speech to Parliament on 24 May 1977, Minister MacKellar set out the basis of Australia's refugee policy to Parliament and established a procedure for assessing applications for refugee status.[53]

In November 1980, when Goodwin-Gill was halfway through his role as UNHCR Legal Adviser in Australia, he spoke at a symposium called 'Refugees: the challenge of the future', organised by the Academy of the Social Sciences in Australia. In this speech he observed that for a nation more accustomed to receiving refugees through formal resettlement programs, the arrival of boats on the northern coastline – and hence a prominent role as a country of 'first asylum' – had 'proved something of a shock' to Australia. And while the number of asylum seekers arriving was small, he said, 'their effect on policy and thinking has been quite exceptional'.[54] Goodwin-Gill was referring specifically to the development of policy and procedure, as mentioned above, as well as Australia's efforts, at that time, to advocate at the international level for creative and principled approaches to the future management of forced migration.[55] But his words could easily have referred to the exceptional effect that boat arrivals had on public anxiety over control of entry, and this book will begin with the story of this public debate. Viviani also spoke at the same symposium, and she made a point of noting that while Australian attitudes to Asian migrants had improved 'radically' with the arrival of the Indochinese refugees, the long-term consequences of this change were yet to be seen, and the final chapter of this book follows how these attitudes evolved.[56]

Over the course of 1976 to 1981 the Vietnamese who made their own way to Australia by boat were brought ashore and given access to permanent settlement. The asylum seekers who arrived just seven years later were received somewhat differently. This book draws on a range of sources to investigate how these things happened and why.

1

Controlling the story

'The boat people had undergone intensive
interviews which had confirmed stories of
hardship and courage.'

*Press release from the Minister for Immigration's
office, 1977*

On a beach in Borneo in April 1976, two men started
talking. One had been at sea for almost forty days with his
younger brother and three friends, having slipped out from
the coastal town of Rach Giá in Southern Vietnam on a
winter's morning. Their patched-up wooden fishing boat,
the *KG4435* or *Kien Giang*, had been reprovisioned and sent
away from port after port along the Gulf of Thailand and the

South China Sea, and now, guided by a page ripped from a school atlas, they were steering north to the Philippines or on to Guam, in the hope that the Americans might fly them to the United States as refugees. His name was Lam Binh, and the story of the five young men's endeavour would be recorded a few years later by scholar of South-East Asian history, My-Van Tran, and published in a slim volume called *The Long Journey: Australia's first boat people*. The other man on the beach was a seasoned Australian sailor, about whom historians know almost nothing. According to the young men's re-telling, the sailor warned they could drown in their attempt to head north. His country had friendly people and had accepted Vietnamese refugees already. It was closer, he said; they should 'take a chance there'.[1]

When Binh hailed the attention of a fisherman near Stokes Hill Wharf in Darwin sixteen days later, on 27 April 1976, around 1200 Vietnamese refugees had already been flown to a new life in Australia, arriving under the Whitlam and Fraser governments.[2] Many had been selected by Australian Department of Immigration officials from temporary camps in and around the places that Binh had sailed through. They landed in Adelaide, Melbourne and Sydney 'without money, clothes or personal belongings', having experienced 'emotional distress and extreme anxiety about their future'.[3] Some were bakers, dressmakers or farmers, and they arrived with an array of languages, religions and levels of education.[4] A few had worked for the Australians during the war, or had close relatives or other connections in the Australian community.

Binh steered into the harbour a stranger. He leant out into the sunshine and in English asked the fisherman if he could speak to the authorities. The next afternoon a spokesperson for the Department of Immigration told the local press that the five young men were being granted one-month temporary entry visas 'while their case was considered' by the Minister. The St Vincent de Paul Society gave the young men a place to stay until they found work on building sites around Darwin, and two Vietnamese-speaking locals helped them to adjust to a new language and culture.

The story of the five's arrival is now seen as a key moment in modern Australian history, their navigation by school atlas a famous detail. Yet, when the story is retold, it is sometimes mentioned that the *Kien Giang* gained little media attention at the time, and did not create 'a local sensation'.[5] In just a few paragraphs the newspapers recounted Binh's story of how and why they had left, and explained that the refugees hoped to gain work as fishermen or mechanics.[6]

The *Kien Giang*'s journey may have been interpreted slightly differently within the Department of Immigration. For almost twelve months Australian authorities had been trying to gain intelligence from within refugee camps across Thailand and Malaysia, hoping to piece together an idea of how Vietnamese refugees were escaping and why.[7] They had received a cable about another group of young men who planned to sail a fishing vessel to Australia if they weren't selected for resettlement by Immigration officials in the region, but that boat never arrived.[8] The Immigration staff who gathered at Stokes Hill Wharf only knew for certain that the five young men who had reached Darwin that day in April 1976 were unprepared and fortunate to have survived the journey in their rickety vessel.

The previous May, when the Department of Labor and Immigration (as it was titled then) had consulted with colleagues in nine other departments to consider how the Whitlam government should respond if a vessel carrying refugees turned up on Australia's northern coastline, they had thought that allowing people to land would create a precedent that 'would not go unremarked by people in a number of countries to the north of Australia'.[9] So if the Australian government couldn't predict or prevent asylum seekers arriving, then it had to shape the story. Years earlier, when Prime Minister Holt's department had debated the fate of stowaways from mainland China in the 1960s, a view was taken that if the government had to let a person stay, it was best to do so 'without publicly demonstrating it'.[10]

The Minister for Immigration's Private Secretary flew to Darwin to see the *Kien Giang*. Wayne Gibbons was relatively young but had experience in the department and had worked for a number of successive Immigration ministers, and the year before he had been dispatched by Whitlam to Guam, Hong Kong and Singapore to select Vietnamese for resettlement. When we spoke in 2011, Gibbons recalled that when he looked at Lam Binh's map and the low-deck vulnerability of the boat, he knew that the young men were incredibly lucky. But he kept in mind past and future head-lines, and the continuing exodus from Vietnam:

> I got sent up there, and our major fear then – I had a very strong fear – was, if we don't handle this well, the mood of the public will become paranoid.

> So we kept it as quiet as we could, it didn't become a big issue, we made people believe it was just a lucky experience for these few men on a boat, they couldn't have done it with a larger group because it was too far a journey[.][11]

For many Vietnamese refugees escape was long in the plan-ning, and more would make the choice to leave their lives behind and clamber aboard a boat months or years after Binh did. More than 2000 people reached Australia over the next six years. From everything we know about their small vessels, it is clear that they were equally lucky, many lacking sailing experience, charts or detailed bearings for their jour-ney.[12] Others still may have tried and failed.

In 1976, less than 10 per cent of migrants who settled in Australia each year were from Asia. Most were from the United Kingdom or its former colonies, with many others

from Southern Europe.[13] They entered to fill specific occu-
pational demands, or as dependents of existing residents.
While a non-discriminatory entry policy had been in place
for several years by now, demographic change was slow to
result after the White Australia Policy was dismantled; in
the midst of an economic downturn the annual immigration intake was recovering from a thirty-year low under the
Whitlam government, and entry criteria were 'more restricted
than those of the 1960s' due to increased unemployment
levels and the Department of Immigration's 'concern for the
employment prospects' of individual migrants.[14] Because
the department had not yet assessed how it would recog-
nise trade or professional qualifications awarded in Asia, it
reported that 'in the present circumstances' migrants from
the region would be mostly confined to family reunion'.[15]

The Minister for Immigration, Michael MacKellar, was
a relatively junior Liberal MP from the Sydney electorate of
Warringah. In his late thirties, he was good-humoured and
self-assured, and had held the role of Shadow Immigration
Minister for a short period in Opposition. After the Coalition won the federal election in December 1975, Fraser
appointed him to a portfolio that was, in MacKellar's words,
considered to be 'low on the totem pole'.[16] The Department
of Immigration had been diminished under the previous
government, and although as noted in the Introduction
the dismantlement of White Australia had been pursued
by key figures within the department, the organisation

was viewed by others as retaining a 'White Australia' mind-set.[17] Whitlam saw the department as 'racist, sexist, narrow and hidebound', and 'totally wedded to the White Australia Policy in all its ramifications'.[18] Fraser said it had a 'latent racism'.[19] MacKellar was tasked with building a holistic approach to migration and social cohesion within the newly reconfigured department, and with increasing support for the Liberal Party among migrant communities.[20] In accordance with the Liberal and National Country Parties' policy platform of August 1975, the department was renamed 'Immigration and Ethnic Affairs'.[21] Scholars have observed that where the Whitlam government promoted a concept of 'multiculturalism' to encourage an openness to cultural difference within Australian society, the policy gained greater momentum in the Fraser years, partly as a consequence of recommendations made through the 'Galbally report' on migrant programs and services.[22] As noted later in this chapter, the increased arrival of Vietnamese refugees by boat from 1977 would make the task of securing party support from migrant communities more complex.

As stated in the Introduction to this book, when the *Kien Giang* arrived, Australia did not have a formal refugee policy or refugee status determination procedure in place. Thus far the Australian government under Whitlam and Fraser had been responding to the Vietnamese and other urgent refugee situations on an ad hoc basis. For instance,

the Lebanese community had urged the government to process thousands of family members fleeing the outbreak of
civil war in Lebanon, and several thousand were brought to
Australia as 'quasi-refugees' on humanitarian grounds in
1975–76. Meanwhile, the Whitlam government had been
caught on the hop by more than 2500 East Timorese who
sailed directly to Darwin in the months before Indonesia invaded their country, and Australia had belatedly and
somewhat reluctantly negotiated with the Portuguese for
them to stay permanently. The young men from the *Kien
Giang* would tell Tran that when they arrived, 'Immigration
neither knew what to do with us nor helped us'.[23] Three
months after they arrived, in July 1976, a spokesperson for
the Department of Immigration told reporters that the five
Vietnamese men now had permanent visas.[24] Until that
point the young men had lived with the worry that they
might be asked to 'move on', and their boat had been sitting anchored in Darwin harbour slowly filling with water.
Before the wet season began Binh was able to bring *Kien
Giang* ashore to repair and then to sell through the local
classifieds.

Later that year it became clear that Vietnamese would
continue to navigate south through the Indonesian archipel-
ago and across the Timor Sea. There was no plan or formal
policy for receiving boats just yet, and as the Minister for
Immigration began to give the media detailed information
about the asylum seekers' journeys and futures, his press

releases presented their arrival as isolated incidents. On the morning of Saturday 28 August 1976, an Australian oil-rig supply vessel, *Lady Cynthia*, rescued a two-month-old baby, eight other children and thirteen adults from a sinking fishing boat off the coast of Indonesia. In keeping with the discretion afforded him as Minister for Immigration, which at that point was unframed by a formal refugee status determination procedure in accordance with Refugee Convention obligations, MacKellar announced that he would offer the refugees 'sanctuary' if they wanted to settle in Australia and met 'acceptable health and character standards'.[25]

According to the press release, most of the adults rescued by the *Lady Cynthia* had a 'working knowledge' of English, and included 'a chemical engineer, an accountant, a bank clerk, typists and students'. When the next two fishing boats managed to reach the safety of Darwin harbour, in late 1976, the story was similar. One boat carried fifty refugees who had fled from the port of Vung Tau, a short distance from Ho Chi Minh City (previously known as Saigon). The 'breadwinners' onboard included an accountant, an optical repairer, a plumber and a mechanic.[26] The second boat arrived just before Christmas, and according to the Minister it too carried breadwinners such as an electrician, a plumber and a carpenter.[27] At 16 metres long this vessel had fifty-six people crammed onboard, and they had been shunted south for almost two months from ports in Malaysia, Thailand, Singapore, Jakarta and Kupang – the Minister described their journey as 'harrowing'. When they reached Darwin, the refugees handed Customs officials a letter they had carefully prepared in English. Their words were included in the press release:

> Please help us for freedom. We live in South Vietnam. Don't want to live with Vietnamese communists […]. We gone to Australia. Please, Australia government help us live in Australia. There are fifty-six persons on board, eighteen mans, ten womans, fourteen boys, fourteen girls. There are ten familys. We shall keep Australia law, will be goodman.

MacKellar described this as 'all that needed to be said'.

For a reader accustomed to a lack of human detail in contemporary Australian asylum policy, in which government press statements announce the interdiction of 'illegal maritime arrivals', it is striking to see these press releases of the 1970s and to be given so many personal details – not just the age and occupation of the refugees, but clues as to how they survived at sea ('only 30 kilograms of rice'), how they navigated the dangerous route ('without maps'), and their immediate needs once they came ashore. It is because of these press releases that these stories of survival are preserved and readily found in online and library collections. One group of seventy-three refugees had drifted west in the Timor Sea and ended up in the remote Cambridge Gulf on

Australia's north-west coastline; among those onboard were a woman who was eight months pregnant, a three-month-old baby, and several small children. Some of the men climbed ashore and trekked inland to a cattle station to alert a rescue party. The Minister publicly explained the schedule of their transfer to a quarantine station in Sydney:

> Our main consideration in making these arrangements is the comfort of these people who have suffered severe hardship on their journey. By shuttling them to Darwin, the refugees will have a full day's rest before flying on to Sydney.[28]

The Department's language was sympathetic but it still conveyed the idea that the federal government was in full control of the refugees' arrival – their reception had been orderly, the press releases said, and proper quarantine procedures had been followed. Cases of tuberculosis were identified, boats were fumigated and any animals the passengers had brought with them were destroyed.[29] 'Everything was being done', the Minister stressed, 'to ensure that the refugees' medical conditions were treated quickly and effectively and that any risk to the community was eliminated'.[30]

The message shifted as time went on and the government became concerned that more Vietnamese refugees might arrive by boat. The Minister's press releases began to speak of the risks facing those who set out on a hazardous journey.[31] The Minister also began to issue warnings that boat people were not guaranteed residence in Australia, a point clearly made for the benefit of both a restless Australian public and for local authorities in Malaysia or Singapore who may have been nudging the refugees onward to Darwin. By the beginning of 1977, only three boats had made it to Australia, but no doubt there were reports of more people on the water in the Gulf of Thailand. On 31 January MacKellar asserted that Australia would likely take a strict approach if the practice of sailing south became 'a large-scale project', although what that new approach might be was unclear.[32] After two small boats reached Broome in May, and just before another three landed on the West Australian coastline, the Minister reiterated 'that any refugee landing in Australia will initially be permitted only to stay temporarily'.[33] Finally, by the end of November 1977, his department had designed a formal procedure for determining refugee status, in which individual boat arrivals would have their claims for protection assessed against criteria under the Refugee Convention, and the Minister for Immigration and the Foreign Minister, Andrew Peacock, publicly clarified that 'genuine refugees would not be turned back'.[34] This line would be maintained until the Vietnamese refugee boats ceased to arrive four years later, in 1981.

In *The Long Journey*, Nancy Viviani described the Fraser government as performing a difficult 'balancing act', navigating competing and disparate pressures in crafting a response to the boats and the broader refugee situation.[35] It is an apt description, because in addition to demand from regional neighbours and the United States for Australia to increase its resettlement program, the government had been caught between the demand from community groups that as a large, sparsely populated country Australia should accept many more refugees, and the resistance of those who accused the government of trying to 'flood' Australia.

Informing the balancing act was the reality that a hard-line response to the refugees would do little for Australia's standing overseas. This was reiterated in public statements by the Ministers for Foreign Affairs and Immigration. At our second meeting in 2011, MacKellar said he had deliberately invoked Australia's international reputation when he spoke at town hall-style meetings or other community events, evidently believing that if Australians could not be moved by 'the humanity of those at sea', then he would have to appeal to their self-image. Photographed speaking with refugee children in Indonesia in mid-1978, when displacement was escalating, the Minister was quoted by the high-circulation magazine the *Australian Women's Weekly* explaining that if the Navy were to turn boats carrying men, women and children around, 'it would take just one well-publicised sinking', 'and our international reputation would be mud'.[36]

Within the government, the Department of Foreign Affairs reiterated concern for the nation's image, part of that department's long-standing interest in improving Australia's standing in the Asian region. In one instance, this concern was in direct response to the actions of the Department of Immigration, when Foreign Affairs expressed deep displeasure that Immigration had disputed Australian responsibility for refugees who arrived after stowing away on a Greek merchant vessel. Foreign Affairs legal advisor Gervase Coles, who would go on to a successful career in UNHCR, argued that the episode drew attention to the treatment of a handful of people 'rather than to our record in the resettlement of 30 000 Indochinese refugees'.[37] It would appear that the 'balancing act' also entailed a tension between Immigration's assertion of control – that only those who 'met Australian requirements' or were found to be 'genuine refugees' would be resettled – and Foreign Affairs' concern for 'the implication of our actions for foreign relations'.

Fraser took a close interest in the work of Foreign Affairs.[38] Talking up the control of entry while emphasising a humane response to refugees fitted within the Prime Minister's noted anti-Communist, anti-racist beliefs and sense of moral obligation toward the Vietnamese, and accorded with the Fraser government's interest in promoting human rights abroad. It also fitted within the government's approach to immigration policy, a progressive and non-discriminatory yet carefully planned system, what sociologist Andrew Jakubowicz has described as a small 'l' liberalism intertwined with a 'conservative concern for social order and social cohesion'.[39] This approach found expression in MacKellar's public assertions that although the Department of Immigration would take 'determined action' against unauthorised boat arrivals, foreshadowing the legislation against the operators of commercialised journeys that was introduced in 1980, the refugees who made landfall were not illegal entrants:[40]

> [....] let me make one thing absolutely clear. The people who have made trips to Australia in small boats are not illegal immigrants. They have made unauthorised trips to Australia but as soon as they arrive they are processed in the normal way and are given valid entry permits, so they are not illegal immigrants. There is a real distinction between those unauthorised arrivals and people within the community who do not hold valid entry permits.[41]

The Minister clarified this point to maintain the appearance of control rather than to assert the legality of claiming asylum, but it set important rhetorical boundaries. His department's annual report for 1978 revisited the point, stating that while the 'boat people had captured headlines', they represented just a tiny number – 'one fortieth' – of the people who were in Australia illegally at that time, such as visa over-stayers or ship deserters, and procedures for their reception were in place:

> The boat people are not illegal entrants. True, persons
> proposed to enter Australia are required to secure a
> visa overseas [...] The boat people do not have visas.
> But on arrival they are interviewed and assessed, and
> their health is checked. They are usually given qualified
> entry permits for temporary residence while their
> claims for permanent residence are assessed in detail.[42]

It would appear, however, that the fact that the boats were few in number was neither here nor there, because the annual report went on to assert that by arriving in the way they did, the asylum seekers challenged 'the adequacy of the *Migration Act* and the resources available to police it', and were therefore 'of enormous concern' to the department.

The balancing act was by no means predetermined. The government was contending with shifting and varied opinions on the boats within the Australian community. Opinion poll data on asylum seekers in this period are limited, but two polls conducted in 1977 and 1979 indicated that around one-quarter to one-third of respondents thought the Fraser government should either stop refugees from arriving by boat or resettle them elsewhere.[43] The majority supported allowing a 'limited number' to stay. However, the Department of Immigration received qualitative evidence directly in the form of correspondence from members of the public expressing opposition to Asian immigration – and according to then Department Secretary Lou Engledow, the authors of these letters were not limited to the Australian-born. Speaking to a conference of academics, advocates and diplomats in Canberra in 1979, Engledow said that discussion of Australia's response to the refugee situation could not ignore the reality that historic anxieties about immigration and racial prejudice still existed within the community, what he called 'the fears under the surface of the Australian mind'.[44]

Higher than usual levels of unemployment heightened concerns that the new arrivals would take something from the existing community to which they were perceived to be unentitled – jobs, resources, and places in the migration program. In 1979 UNHCR's Legal Adviser, Dr Goodwin-Gill, reported to UNHCR that there was public opposition to an increase in the overall immigration program because of conditions within the Australian economy.[45] This is perhaps why MacKellar's public statements referred to the refugees' occupations, as noted earlier, and contained reassurances that government would 'balance the claims of compassion and humanity with the needs of the workplace'.[46]

Public attitudes toward the refugee intake were part of a larger debate about the future of Australia's immigration program, which the Department of Immigration was recalibrating in size and structure at this same time. It is beyond the scope of this book to examine this wider policy context (and it has been detailed by Freda Hawkins and James Jupp, among others), but a point to make here is that, as the department acknowledged in its 1977 Green Paper on Immigration Policies and Australia's Population, some established migrant communities feared that refugees were usurping the place of their loved ones in obtaining entry to Australia.[47] A First Assistant Secretary in the Department of Immigration at the time, Derek Volker, was closely involved in producing the Green Paper, a process in which the department had liaised with employers, the labour movement, and migrant communities. He recalled that people waiting to bring relatives in through the migration program felt that it was unfair that refugees arriving by boat were being accepted: 'Suddenly you've got people turning up [and migrant communities are] saying, "How are these people getting in?", "They're taking over the country" sort of thing, "we can't get our relatives in"'.[48] Australian Council of Trade Unions President and future prime minister Bob Hawke gave credence to this sense of unfairness when he decried that 'illegal immigrants', including Vietnamese boat refugees, were being accepted while family reunion applicants were subject to more restrictive assessment.[49] When the Minister for Immigration presented the results of the departmental consultations to Parliament in June 1978, he sought to stem the criticism by acknowledging 'shortcomings' in the administration of family entry.[50]

A negative public perception that refugees were taking up space in the migration program persisted nonetheless, as the refugee resettlement program increased, and the Minister was forced to again point out that the family and humanitarian streams were separate, and 'there can be no suggestion that more of one means less of another'.[51] But as the displacement in Indochina grew in size and political complexity from 1978 on, and Australia's resettlement program increased, the Department of Immigration's own terminology became caught up in a comparison between those within the refugee stream, and the idea that refugees arriving by boat were 'queue-jumping' refugees selected from the camps, and this term was subsequently echoed by the Labor Party.[52] Labor MPs also argued that a focus on Indochinese refugees denied a 'fair share' of Australia's resettlement places to refugees elsewhere in the world, and the trade union movement was agitating for the plight of activists fleeing rightist regimes in Latin America (a cause Labor would pursue on winning office in 1983).[53]

Some opposition to the Vietnamese arriving by boat went beyond questions of fairness, and reflected geographic insecurity and racial prejudice. A group calling itself the Immigration Control Association distributed leaflets in the suburbs of Melbourne that reminded readers of the Japanese offensive against Australia in the Second World War, and claimed that Fraser and MacKellar were 'actually encouraging the new (peaceful) Asian invasion threatening to overwhelm us'.[54] In 1979, the Commissioner for Community Relations, former Whitlam Minister for Immigration Al Grassby, reportedly identified at least thirty organisations 'with racist aims' operating in Australia.[55] In fringe-group literature and the pages of major national newspapers alike, Vietnamese refugees were accused, variously, of being 'Communist agents', 'pirates, brothel keepers and drug runners', or the harbingers of a 'tide of human flotsam' that could flood Australia's northern coastline. Goodwin-Gill observed 'intemperate' and 'ill-informed' characterisations of the refugees cropping up in national debate, and in 1979 he reported back to UNHCR that there remained within the Australian community a 'considerable hostility to the idea of an Asian intake'.[56] For his part the Minister remembered being labelled 'Yella MacKellar'. When he sat with me in 2010 he talked over the public response to the boats:

> [...] in public meetings and things [...] They'd say, 'you're bloody mad, why don't you go out there, we've got a Navy, go out there and if they won't go home blast them out of the water?!' And I'd say, 'Oh, that's terrific, yeah that'd look really good on international television wouldn't it? The Australian Navy firing on unprotected ships with women and children on board. It'd look really good!'[57]

At the same time, some community groups and individuals were accusing the Minister of lacking generosity because he insisted that only 'genuine' refugees would be allowed to stay. With a population of only 14 million, surely Australia had land and resources to spare? The arguments stretched beyond Australia's involvement in Vietnam all the way back to the origins of European settlement. 'It was a good thing', the Australian Council for Overseas Aid told the media, that 'the Aboriginal community had not had a person like Mr MacKellar among its members when Captain Phillip arrived with the First Fleet'.[58]

Nowhere was this balancing act more important than in the lead-up to the December 1977 federal election, a campaign that began in the midst of a sharp increase in the number of refugees reaching the Northern Territory coastline. The language of 'invasion' and vocal suspicions about the refugees' motivations made headlines at home and in the region; Singapore's *Straits Times* observed that where once Darwin was 'a port of hospitality', refugees were now seen as 'a pain in the neck'.[59] From politicians in Darwin to UN officials in Sydney, public anxieties about the boats did not go unnoticed. Concerns ranged from the implications for quarantine (particularly in relation to livestock), the adequacy of coastal surveillance and the perceived economic risks of unregulated, unplanned entry.[60]

Some within the Labor Party had assumed that because the Vietnamese resettled thus far in Australia were fleeing the aftermath of the communist victory, they had therefore 'all raced off to join the Liberal Party', and doubted whether these people could really be refugees.[61] Labor senator Tony Mulvihill aired suspicions that some were 'black marketeers', and claimed that if the Labor Party won government, boat refugees could be sent back to the camps.[62] This sentiment was shared not only within parts of the labour movement – the Darwin branch of the Waterside Workers Federation announced stop-work actions in protest at the boats – but also by some on the conservative side of politics. The Northern Territory leader Paul Everingham, of the Country Liberal Party, confirmed in the Legislative Assembly that Australia should take many refugees through orderly processes and a 'determined stand' against those arriving on their own.[63] Everingham reportedly wrote to Prime Minister Fraser demanding that the Australian Navy be dispatched to the Timor and Arafura seas to turn back any Vietnamese at sea. 'They've just got to be stopped', Everingham told the press. 'There is no way we can handle an invasion of this magnitude, even if it is peaceful.'[64]

When compared with recent Australian history, this election campaign stands out. Scholars such as Neumann, Viviani and others have noted that in the beginning of the campaign the government was slow to respond to the language of 'invasion' and to calls to stop the boats. A month in, and during a week in which seven boats arrived carrying 259 people, it was forced to take a stronger position.[65] The shift was strategic, not least because a hardened line in national politics did little to strengthen Australia's position with host countries in the region. Thus the 126 men, forty-four women and eighty-nine children who arrived in that seven-day period in mid-November 'did not pose a threat to the Australian community', MacKellar announced, and 'were indeed homeless people seeking a new country in which to settle'.[66] The photos on the front cover of this book may have been intended to carry that message; one depicts a young child, Xye Than Hue, in the arms of Customs officer Frank Dalton, and was taken at the wharf during that hectic week in Darwin by Michael Jensen, an official photographer with the Australian Information Service. Jensen's photos are a small black and white collection now in the National Library of Australia, and capture four wooden craft with large lettering on their sides – the *VNSG053*, *PK3402*, *VNKG0395* and the *VNKG1062*, all of which arrived the same day. The boats are anchored alongside each other, with babies toddling on the decks in the sunshine and young men gathering as My-Van Tran (working as an interpreter), Immigration officer Ian Marks and other staff in short-sleeved shirts, shorts and long socks step aboard to start initial paperwork.

It is worth quoting here parts of a press release issued by the Minister's office on 25 November 1977 to get a sense of how the government explained these latest arrivals to the public:

> Mr MacKellar said there was no factual basis to claims that many of the Vietnamese were wealthy people of dubious character. The boat people had undergone intensive interviews which had confirmed stories of hardship and courage.

The few who had gold in their possession seemed anything but wealthy. All had come from an unstable area in which gold had been long recognised as the only real possession of monetary value.[67]

Once again, those on board included 'mechanics, welders, farmers, teachers, managers, cleaners, nurses, carpenters', and small details gave Australians a glimpse into their experience:

The 56 year old woman [...] had bought the boat from her brother, a fisherman, who had tried to escape with her but had been caught and imprisoned. Her eldest son, a deaf mute, had skippered the 45 ton vessel part of the way [...]

Finally, the appeal went beyond any sense of moral responsibility to the Vietnamese and instead looked outward, to the nation's status abroad:

Mr MacKellar said: 'Australia, in accepting these people, is honouring its international obligations to provide sanctuary to refugees. I am confident that the Australian community will continue to support the Government's efforts in helping these people to make a new life in a new and hospitable land.'

The press release was trying to say as much about its audience as it was about the refugees, in an attempt to tap into the average person's perception of themselves and their country. This high-minded focus on the refugees' individual experiences and the appeal to hospitality was essentially the government's only option as it tried to avoid politicising the refugee issue. The press release is a good example of what Viviani has called an attempt by 'a somewhat reluctant government' to 'soft-pedal' the issue and 'defuse the hysterical element in public debate which, at times, looked dangerously likely to degenerate into openly racist hostility'.[68]

The tone was tested when, four days later (and twelve days before voters went to the polls), 175 refugees reached Australia aboard a 50-metre trawler called the _Song Be 12_. The passengers had wrested control of the vessel from Vietnamese soldiers and crew, some of whom were reportedly still held hostage when the allegedly hijacked trawler moored in Darwin. The day the vessel arrived the Ministers for Immigration and Foreign Affairs released a joint statement emphasising that the refugee boats 'must not be allowed' to become an issue in the campaign, 'because', they argued, 'the basic question of human suffering transcends partisan advantage', and because 'Australia's status in the region would be seriously – and justifiably – damaged if it were'.[69]

In our interview, former Prime Minister Fraser said he 'wasn't conscious' of the refugee situation 'being a major issue' during the 1977 campaign. This was because, he said, 'we still weren't playing politics with [it]', a view surely informed by hindsight and the nature of contemporary political debate on asylum seekers. Fraser said his attentions during the 1977 campaign were absorbed elsewhere, in a scandal over land speculation involving Treasurer Phillip Lynch.[70] The Treasurer's downfall might have been front-page news, but so too was public opinion on the *Song Be 12*. '"Stop the Refos" is the cry in Darwin', read the headline on page one of the *Canberra Times*, atop a vox-pop piece in which patrons at one of Darwin's pubs expressed their frustration at refugees suspected of hijacking and 'sneaking in through the back door'.[71] The patrons' resentment mixed with the economic issues at the heart of that election, a campaign centred on tax cuts and unemployment.[72] It was not a matter 'of racialism or not being humanitarian', those interviewed clarified, 'we've got unemployment raging, a government that is hell bent on cutting spending' and yet that government is 'virtually sticking out their hand' to the refugees 'and saying welcome'.

The arrival of the *Song Be 12* was not simply a matter for the Department of Immigration, but a matter for Foreign Affairs, as representatives of the Vietnamese government disputed the passengers' refugee status in the Australian press. The Australian Foreign Minister Andrew Peacock carefully announced that if the boat was the property of the Socialist Republic of Vietnam (SRV) it could be returned, and reiterated the line that 'genuine refugees' could stay.[73] Most of those aboard the *Song Be 12* were flown to Sydney a few days later, in the midst of vocal comment by some members of the Labor Party.[74] Allegations of 'piracy' by the SRV played into the already prejudicial conceptions of the Vietnamese refugees that were circulating amongst the political 'Left'. Unwilling to return passengers to a potential risk of harm, but quite rattled by their method of flight, MacKellar took the line that to question the bona fides of those who were fleeing Vietnam was 'a slur on the refugees themselves' and 'an unwarranted slur' on other countries who were accepting them for resettlement.[75]

In the days leading up to the poll, at which the Fraser government would be returned to office, MacKellar released more statements attempting to emphasise the quality of health screening for refugees and the rigour of interview procedures and coastal surveillance, and to assert that Australia 'will continue to meet our international obligations' to refugees. As a First Assistant Secretary, Volker was working closely with the Minister. He remembered 'afternoons spent writing press releases, telling everyone we were in control'.[76] The *Song Be 12*'s suspect origins continued to make headlines for weeks afterward, well into the following year, as the return of the vessel and voluntary return of some of the crew were negotiated with the SRV. Immigration staff privately observed that hijackings were 'of growing community concern in Australia', and a disquiet about the boat's provenance, both within the public and the department, helped inform the government's desire to take a hard line when large commercialised escapes from Vietnam became an issue in late 1978.[77]

In his expert history *From White Australia to Woomera*, James Jupp argues that despite a long record of resettling refugees, most Australians have no real sense of what it means to be displaced, and thus 'cannot be expected to fully understand experiences which they have never witnessed and which have never impinged on Australia'.[78] It was perhaps this reading of the public mind that drove the Department of Immigration and Ethnic Affairs to set out in its annual report of 1978 that 'it is sobering to consider how easily today's well-established and confident citizen can, by the overnight imposition of an unacceptable political and economic regimen, become tomorrow's refugee'.[79] Within the department staff proposed creating displays at Australian consulates abroad that could promote the nation's refugee history, and materials to inform Australians about 'the nature and size of the problem and the very real humanitarian issues involved'.[80] Managing public disquiet entailed a media strategy. When MacKellar was in Indonesia in mid-1978 attempting to convince the Suharto government to allow boats to land and not continue their journey south, he was accompanied by journalist Keith Finlay from the *Australian Women's Weekly*. Finlay wrote a sympathetic feature story about forty-one Vietnamese floundering in a boat off the edge of Timor who had sent a letter to the Australian Embassy in Jakarta asking for sanctuary, and the piece captured the government's message well. Interspersed with warm family photos of refugees, the article told how 'hurried inter-governmental talks' ensured the women, men and thirteen children were allowed to disembark and be processed for resettlement rather than risk 'murderous seas' on their fourth attempt to sail to Australia.[81]

The size and extent of the refugee situation became a key part of the message by late 1978 and into 1979. At the end of 1978, UNHCR's Sydney office made note that the Department of Immigration and Ethnic Affairs was using visual materials to 'dramatise the refugee situation in South-East Asia […] and create a groundswell of public opinion' in favour of the resettlement effort.[82] During a week in April 1979 when more than 200 refugees made it to Darwin, MacKellar made headlines by claiming that half of all those who fled Vietnam 'had drowned or died in other ways'.[83] In September that year, Sydney-based commercial radio station 2UE featured a 60-minute report on the plight of Indochinese refugees in Thailand and Hong Kong, followed by an extended talk-back segment with the Minister for Immigration and Ethnic Affairs. It was reported in the press the next day that of sixteen listeners who dialled in to question the Minister, only four supported Australia's refugee program. Other callers said the report about the refugees had been 'emotive' but they 'were not moved at all', and claimed they were in the 'vast majority' of Australians who did not support taxpayer-funded resettlement. One question was: 'What has happened to the White Australia Policy?' (to which the Minister replied 'We haven't got one'), which highlights just how recent – and fragile – the end of racially discriminatory immigration policy was at that time. Another listener asked what would happen when the Vietnamese refugees who settled in Australia 'multiply in the future?'.[84]

Within the Labor Party, a shift of some sort had occurred. MPs considered the refugees now fleeing Vietnam to be distinct from (and somehow more deserving than) the Vietnamese who had fled after the fall of Saigon, who were (still) perceived as wealthy and ideologically opposed to the labour movement. Mick Young told the Labor Party's National Conference in 1979 that 'the attitudes of a lot of us, including myself, have changed very much on this question of refugees from South-East Asia', and in so doing he repeated erroneous ideas about the refugees who had previously fled Vietnam:

> I do not think in our wildest dreams anyone could
> have described or referred to the first batch that came
> from Vietnam as being refugees as they arrived in
> Australia with their gold bars and servants and general's
> uniforms. [...] but the people leaving Vietnam and
> other areas of South-East Asia today are refugees.[85]

Young took the view that in light of the many thousands of Indochinese refugees hosted in the Asian region, Australia had little choice but to resettle the small number of Vietnamese who arrived directly. By 1980 Young was Shadow Minister for Immigration, and as Australia's intake remained high during 1980–82, he accompanied MacKellar's successor as Minister, Ian Macphee, to public meetings at which they sought to explain the non-discriminatory refugee and immigration program to the community.[86] Following the 1980 federal election, which saw the Fraser government returned to office, the newly appointed Secretary of the Department of Immigration and Ethnic Affairs, John Menadue, would credit this bipartisanship for helping to ensure 'there was no significant opposition' to the refugee intake during the campaign.[87]

Two years after he had reached Australia, Lam Binh was based in Brisbane and was working at a factory. By now he had sold the *Kien Giang*, but the resilience and endeavour of that voyage had inspired him to dream of bigger things. In January 1978 he travelled down to Canberra to try to convince the Department of Immigration to approve his parents, two brothers and two sisters for resettlement in Australia. The family were reportedly living in a hut in a refugee camp near the border between Thailand and Laos. Now that he was settled, Binh hoped they could be reunited.

Then, he told the *Canberra Times*, he dreamt of buying a new boat and circumnavigating the globe.[88]

At that very same time, Australian authorities reported that it was common for Vietnamese families to split up as they fled, to disperse the risk of their uncertain journey and because they were holding on to the idea that they might see one another again.[89] Binh's family members had initially fled aboard the *Kien Giang* with him, his brother Lam Tac Tam and three companions, but, seasick and uncertain about what lay ahead, they had disembarked in Thailand and said their goodbyes with the same hopes of ultimately being reunited. It would take until 1980 for the family to move to Australia, via Canada, but Binh was tragically killed in a car accident in Brisbane before they arrived. Another of the men from the *Kien Giang* died with him.[90] Lam Tac Tam settled in Darwin and in 2016 he featured in a campaign created by UNHCR's Canberra office called 'Human Lives, Human Rights', alongside former refugees from Afghanistan, Iran and Iraq who had reached Australia by boat years after he did and were placed in Woomera or Curtin detention centres. Posing with his children and grandchildren, he told the interviewer 'today [you] help someone, tomorrow someone help you'.[91]

The author Carina Hoang has written eloquently of the fate, known or unknown, of the one and a half million Vietnamese who fled their country during the 1970s, 1980s, and into the 1990s, preserving the memory of those who perished in camps or on the water, and telling the stories of those who made it to a country of resettlement and 'have struggled to put their pain and sorrows behind them' as they built a new life.[92] More than 100 000 refugees from Vietnam, as well as Laos and Cambodia, were resettled in Australia by 1985, and tens of thousands more by the mid-1990s.[93] Reflecting on the successful outcomes of Vietnamese resettlement, and the hard work and sacrifice involved in building a future in Australia, My-Van Tran wrote in 2001 that 'the Vietnamese sense of gratitude is deep', and there exists a sense of 'moral obligation' within the community to 'give back to their adoptive country'.[94] For Ian Macphee that gratitude has gone both ways. Having overseen the height of Australia's Indochinese resettlement as Minister for Immigration and Ethnic Affairs from late 1979 to 1982, he has maintained close ties with the Vietnamese community in Australia. In 2012, thirty years after leaving the portfolio, Macphee was invited to address the community's 21st national conference, held in the western suburbs of Sydney, and he told his audience, 'you have enriched my life'.[95]

This resettlement program was far from predetermined. The Fraser government's acceptance of refugees from Vietnam, as well as from Laos and Cambodia, was initially halting and incremental. The demographer Charles A Price argued that Australia had been 'caught flat-footed' by the displacement from Vietnam, with no discernible idea 'as to how non-discriminatory refugee policy should work'.[96]

Nancy Viviani wrote that while the Fraser government embarked on 'an initial show of altruism' in accepting small numbers of Vietnamese after taking office, it resisted public and international pressure for a much greater intake until it became clear that boats would arrive more regularly, and other scholars have argued resettlement got underway with the need to secure 'boat-holding' arrangements with host countries in the region (a subject that will be discussed in chapter 3 of this book).[97] The intake was indeed slow at first – just over 2000 Indochinese were selected in the region and flown to Australia for resettlement in 1977. This grew to more than 9000 the year after, and then finally to a high of more than 15 000 in both 1980 and 1981.[98] Notwithstanding the explanations cited above, the intake should also be viewed against the backdrop of a gradually increasing immigration program, which, as stated earlier, was being revived from a record low of 52 000 settlers under Whitlam to well over 118 000 in the early 1980s.

Michael MacKellar had told Parliament in 1977 that Indochinese refugees would be welcomed 'at a level consistent with our capacity as a community to resettle them'.[99] It was a common refrain but judgments of this capacity differed, both within public debate and within (and between) governments. In late 1975, a Senate inquiry began to hear competing assessments from community and religious organisations and government agencies as to Australia's capacity to respond to Vietnamese refugees. The Department of the Prime Minister and Cabinet under the Whitlam government gave evidence that Australia's capacity to accept refugees was 'not unlimited':

> There are limits beyond which, for economic and social
> reasons, it would be imprudent to go. Where these
> limits are located is necessarily a question of judgment
> and, therefore, often perhaps a matter of dispute.[100]

Prime Minister and Cabinet acknowledged that in exercising this judgment, and selecting refugees and other humanitarian entrants, 'there will always be people who are disappointed'. The Senate Committee's findings echoed this point.

As the refugee and immigration intake were being developed, through 1977 to 1979, practical capacity was an issue for some: in internal discussions, the Department of Finance warned that an increased refugee intake would 'add to the overall unemployment problem and increase the budget deficit', and the already high quota was 'placing strains on services provided for migrants'.[101] The launch of a Community Refugee Settlement Scheme by the department in 1979 sought to offset some of these initial reception costs while attempting to harness public goodwill, enabling organisations or individuals within the Australian community to provide assistance to newly resettled Indochinese refugees.

Some observers suspected, however, that ideas about

material capacity also mixed with the less tangible but more political impacts of change in the community, what the *New York Times* observed as a 'residual anti-Asian racism' in the Australian community.[102] The academic Robert Manne wrote in 1978 that the reason the resettlement program took some years to gain momentum was because the boats had 'activated our deepest collective neurosis'. It was timidity on the part of 'our government and administrators', he argued, a fear that bringing in non-white refugees in large numbers would create social (or political) problems, and it ran subcutaneously through press coverage and politicians' responses.[103]

Manne's assessment wasn't necessarily unwarranted. Indeed, the capacity of the Australian community to accept demographic change – so close on the heels of a 'White Australia' and in the midst of higher than usual unemployment – was identified in both internal and external government publications as a factor in the management of the refugee program. For example, Macphee actively promoted the Community Refugee Settlement Scheme as a way to promote public understanding of refugee issues. What is most interesting, however, is the distinction between community acceptance of planned refugee resettlement from Indochina, and the response to Vietnamese boat arrivals. In 1978 MacKellar submitted to Cabinet that the community might not support an increase in the refugee intake, and in response Fraser's Department of Prime Minister and Cabinet suggested that the Minister be asked to explain the grounds for his assumption. From the view of that department, 'the main thrust of any public criticism seems to be directed against boat arrivals', whereas those refugees selected from the region and brought to Australia 'appear to arouse little comment'.[104] In just two years, people seeking protection directly had become a focal point for community anxieties, and would retain this in subsequent decades.

In *The Long, Slow Death of White Australia*, Gwenda Tavan writes that Asian immigration and other social reforms of the 1970s in areas such as Aboriginal affairs and the promotion of multiculturalism 'forced Australians to confront, once and for all, the practical consequences of the bipartisan decision [...] to abolish racial discrimination in public policy'.[105] The confrontation was made more difficult by Australia's role in receiving those refugees who risked the boat journey south, and not just an accustomed role as a country of planned resettlement. If the Indochinese refugee intake was the first test of the end of White Australia, as it is popularly considered to be, then the government and public response to boat arrivals was part of this challenge.

The last group of Vietnamese refugees to sail to Australia during the Fraser era landed just before Easter 1981, but the number of boats had decreased markedly almost two years earlier, around mid-1979. In December that year MacKellar was replaced by Macphee and moved on to the Health portfolio. Although MacKellar would later step down from Health due to a controversy over a failure to properly declare the importation of a colour television, he enjoyed reflecting on his appointment to that portfolio, which he considered to be a mark of his success in Immigration. According to his anecdote, he had been having dinner at a restaurant in Sydney one evening in late 1979 when a waiter had approached the table with a message: 'The Prime Minister's on the phone'. The government was preparing to go to the polls the following year, and cuts to universal health insurance had proved contentious. In MacKellar's re-telling, Fraser 'wanted everything dampened down'. Between the chatter of diners and the clang of steaming pots, MacKellar stood beside the kitchen with the receiver to his ear and was told he had a new role, because 'I had a bit of a reputation for – evidently – for keeping the lid on difficult situations'.[106]

2

Recognised as refugees

'[The procedures] enable a State to identify those who should benefit from international protection under the Convention, and those who should not.'

UNHCR

In October 1977 the Executive Committee of the UNHCR held its annual meeting at the Palais des Nations in Geneva. Known as 'ExCom', the Committee is a subsidiary organ of the United Nations General Assembly, and its members are states and UN specialised agencies. At this meeting, member states noted serious displacement in southern Africa and Latin America and the 'dramatic' situation evolving in Indochina. ExCom discussed the need for states parties to the Refugee Convention to set up procedures for assessing individual refugee claims. It was noted that 'only a limited number' of states had procedures in place at that time – less than half the thirty-one represented in the room. Under ExCom Conclusion No. 8 Determination of Refugee Status, ExCom recommended that states have 'a single central authority' responsible for making an initial decision on refugee claims, and if that decision was negative the applicant should be given time to appeal through either the courts or an administrative authority. ExCom hoped that states would 'give favourable consideration' to UNHCR participation in this decision making process.[1]

Such procedures – when fair, efficient and principled – are essential to the fulfilment of states' obligations under the Convention, because they can protect a person from being sent back to persecution (under the principle of '*non-refoulement*') by determining whether they meet the definition of 'refugee' under Article 1A(2) of the treaty. As UNHCR puts it, the procedures 'enable a State to identify those who should benefit from international protection under the Convention, and those who should not'.[2] A refugee is defined as someone who, 'owing to well-founded fear of being persecuted for reasons of race, religion, nationality, membership of a particular social group or political opinion, is outside the country of his nationality and is unable or, owing to such fear, is unwilling to avail himself of the protection of that country'. An asylum seeker 'is someone who is seeking protection as a refugee', but has not yet had their claim determined.[3]

Australia was one of the member states at ExCom that did not have a status determination procedure in place at that time. Even the number of people who had sought asylum in Australia had not been recorded consistently until this point.[4] But planning was now underway, and as delegates addressed the room in turn, the Australian representative took the floor and described the refugee policy that his government had announced earlier that year, through which Australia would be able to admit and resettle more refugees. In his Ministerial Statement on Refugee Policy (24 May 1977), the Minister for Immigration had told Parliament that 'Australia has accepted certain obligations in relation to people covered by the Convention', and:

> Situations arise from time to time in which people
> [...] [in Australia] claim to be refugees entitled to the
> protection of the Convention [...] A standing inter-
> departmental body will be established to evaluate such
> claims and to make recommendations on them to me.
> It is proposed that the Office of the UNHCR will be
> involved as necessary in these deliberations.[5]

Before and after ExCom, on more than half a dozen occasions in the second half of 1977, senior Immigration officials met with the UNHCR and other government departments and planned how the procedure would work. They discussed which departments would have a representative on a new decision making body known as the Determination of Refugee Status Committee (known as 'DORS'), and determined that there would be representatives from Immigration, Foreign Affairs, Attorney-General's, and Prime Minister and Cabinet. Foreign Affairs was included because that department considered applications for refugee status to be of 'paramount foreign policy significance'.[6] The Department of Prime Minister and Cabinet was included to oversee decision making, and if necessary to question the political or legal advice provided by other committee members.[7] The Attorney-General's representative was to be a senior solicitor from the human rights branch of that department, interested in procedural fairness.[8] Two Immigration officials would attend DORS, one to chair (and cast a deciding vote if necessary), and the other to vote alongside their fellow members.

It was also agreed that UNHCR would attend DORS meetings in an advisory, non-voting capacity, acting as an observer to the integrity of proceedings and offering expert advice on conditions in countries of origin and on international law. Six years later, in one of the first comparative studies of status determination procedures across Europe, North America and Australia, published in the *Stanford Journal of International Law*, the author Christopher L Avery reported that the 'active inclusion' of

UNHCR at the decision making level in Canberra was 'the most important positive feature of the Australian system'.[9] UNHCR's direct participation would cease once the government replaced DORS with another form of decision making in 1990, part of broader changes that I will discuss in chapter 6 of this book.

When the planning meetings for DORS began in 1977, it was not a given that the Vietnamese would be assessed in the same way that other asylum seekers were.[10] The records show that other alternatives were posed: should the boat arrivals be required to apply for protection? Or should they be processed through a separate procedure? The Immigration official who chaired these planning meetings, First Assistant Secretary Derek Volker, thought it was best that all refugees who arrived at Australia's borders submit an application for protection, 'for consistency of approach'.[11] A Cabinet decision of 16 March 1978 endorsed this policy.[12]

The act of recognising or rejecting a person's claim for protection requires careful application of the Convention definition of 'refugee', to determine who is a person with a well-founded fear of persecution, for reasons of their race, religion, nationality, political opinion or membership of a particular social group. It is a task that requires, and arguably improves with, training and experience. The Deputy Director of the UNHCR Division of International Protection, Ivor C Jackson, met with Immigration during the planning stages for DORS in 1977 and reported back to

Geneva that 'the work of the Committee in its early stages will call for more intensive UNHCR participation, in view of the numerous questions of principle and procedure which will need to be clarified'.[13]

During these planning meetings UNHCR had also observed that the Department of Immigration was looking to apply 'very liberal criteria' to applicants, and 'the overriding consideration seems to be whether the person concerned would be confronted – irrespective of the actual reasons for his departure – with serious difficulties if returned to his country of origin'.[14]

This may seem an unexpected position for the Immigration department to take, given that internal departmental papers had described those who sailed to Australia as 'self-selecting' and bypassing 'official procedure'.[15] But the approach was consistent with the department's understanding of conditions in the SRV. During the planning sessions in late 1977, Immigration had acknowledged it was unlikely that Vietnamese boat arrivals could be sent back.[16] From what UNHCR observed in those sessions, 'Australian authorities believed that, in the final analysis, they would have no option but to permit the persons concerned to remain in Australia'.[17]

Under the 'Rules of Procedure' for DORS, which the government finalised in early 1978, Vietnamese boat arrivals and asylum seekers from any other country who arrived in any other manner would be assessed against the criteria set out in the Refugee Convention (as a matter of law) and against broader humanitarian considerations (as a sign of goodwill).[18] The latter was a discretionary form of additional assistance, described here as 'compassionate/humanitarian leave to remain', that had been adopted in various forms by several states parties by this time, and it aligned with the Minister's pledge that government policy would be 'sufficiently flexible' for people who fell outside the strict Convention definition.[19]

The final decision on a person's claim would sit with the Minister for Immigration. Rejected applicants would have no formal right of appeal, but the Minister could refer their case back to the Committee for reconsideration. This was not ideal, as the ExCom Conclusion emphasised, but it was in keeping with Australia's long-standing approach to entry, in which, as Mary Crock has observed, control 'is recognised as an incident of state sovereignty'.[20] Indeed, while recognising Australia's 'humanitarian commitment and responsibility to admit refugees for resettlement' was first among the Minister's stated principles of refugee policy, a close second was that 'the decision to accept refugees must always remain with the Government of Australia'.[21]

The asylum seekers who sailed to Australia before March 1978 were granted temporary entry permits, as Lam Binh and his brother and companions had been, and later the Minister told Parliament that these refugees had been accepted as permanent settlers.[22] They numbered 1043 people. Those who came ashore after March were told that they would have to submit individual applications for refugee status to DORS. They numbered roughly 1035 people between 1978 and 1981 (when the last boat of this 'wave' arrived). Of these, the overwhelming majority were from Vietnam; only two are listed as hailing from Laos and Cambodia, which is consistent with other records on the boat arrivals at this time.[23] Australia's formal procedure for assessing individual claims for protection began to operate in March 1978.

When mentioned at all in histories of Vietnamese settlement in Australia, the DORS Committee has usually been viewed as a reaction to a political problem, presented as a way to fulfil obligations but designed for domestic reasons.[24] In reality, DORS was a necessary part of Australia's obligations under the Convention and Protocol, just as other states parties to those instruments – such as Canada and New Zealand – were engaged in setting up their own procedures at this time.[25]

That said, the committee's formation was nonetheless 'exacerbated' (as the Department of Prime Minister and Cabinet put it) by the arrival of Vietnamese in northern Australia and after 'prodding' by that department.[26] It fitted within the Liberal and National Country Party policy platform of August 1975, and the Senate Committee

recommendations of 1976, which had called for the creation
of mechanisms to respond to urgent refugee situations. And
for the Department of Immigration and Ethnic Affairs,
the procedure served an important political purpose. Just
before the committee began operation, in February 1978,
MacKellar had told Cabinet that DORS would allow the
government to defend itself against claims that the boat
arrivals did not merit Australia's protection:

> Some criticism may also come from those who deny
> that the people involved are refugees at all in the
> accepted international sense. It will be necessary
> to point to measures that are taken to verify their
> refugee status, including through the Committee on
> Determination of Refugee Status.[27]

The Minister could then proceed to acknowledge public
concerns about the credibility of those arriving by boat, and
assure people that a rigorous procedure was in place to check
who was 'genuine' and who wasn't:

> One thing we have to guard against is the possibility
> that some people who do not have a well-founded fear
> of persecution […] will seek to use the refugee outflow
> as a means of migrating to Australia when they would
> not normally qualify […] Those who have arrived in
> Australia without prior authority […] are interviewed

very closely about their past, their departure from
Vietnam and their reasons for leaving [...].[28]

One of MacKellar's press releases said that these interviews
'are considered by the Determination of Refugee Status
Committee which advises me on whether the application
should be given refugee status'.[29] Whether the Minister's
message made a difference to community opinion is another
matter. The efficacy of the DORS process had been publicly
questioned at least as early as May 1978, just two months
after it began, when muttered accusations from anonymous
intelligence officials appeared in the Australian press to the
effect that 'once boatpeople appear off the coast, their arrival
is a fait accompli', and DORS scrutiny of their claims was
'severely limited'.[30] But in focusing on these procedures,
MacKellar was trying to emphasise that he, as Minister for
Immigration, had ultimate control over who stayed in Australia and who did not.

DORS has long been but a footnote to the story of
successful Vietnamese resettlement in Australia, a story that
played out in the media, in the community, parliament
and the Cabinet. Some government records are available in
the National Archives of Australia, but thanks to studious
note-taking by UNHCR officials it is possible to see what
happened more systematically, when DORS read, discussed
and decided upon these individual applications for refugee
status. These files offer a consistent record of 92 meetings

from October 1978 to April 1983, spanning the four and a half years Goodwin-Gill worked in Australia. They show that once a status determination procedure was announced in Parliament and in the Palais des Nations, another chapter in the story of Australia's response to the Vietnamese then began amongst a group of six people, in a conference room, behind the scenes in Canberra.

On 10 October 1978, the UNHCR Regional Representative Gilberto Rizzo and Dr Goodwin-Gill landed in crisp sunshine at Canberra airport. They were there to attend Goodwin-Gill's first DORS Committee meeting, in his role as the new UNHCR Legal Adviser in Australia. The committee were set to consider the cases of eight Vietnamese who had sailed to Australia earlier in the year. The applicants had fled for a variety of reasons, including fear of being sent to re-education camps, or their military service under the previous government. One man had made it out on his second attempt, and skippered the escape boat with his wife alongside him. Their stories were typical of the tens of thousands of refugees who fled Vietnam at that time.

DORS members did not normally interview applicants themselves, but instead relied on the transcripts of interviews, conducted by Immigration officials after refugees had successfully anchored in Darwin harbour or arrived off Australia's remote northern coastline and were moved to accommodation.[31] Alongside their personal details, ethnicity, religion, occupation and personal background, individuals were asked their reasons for leaving Vietnam and why they did not want to return.[32] Both the skills of the interviewers and the questions they posed initially yielded ambiguous or incomplete answers. This meant that when DORS began its work in March 1978, the Committee was struggling to assess the credibility of applicants and their fear of persecution, and were unsure 'just how the answers should be interpreted'.[33] In August 1978, before Goodwin-Gill arrived in Australia, another UNHCR representative, Mr E Solomon, had attended committee meetings and reported that DORS members doubted 'the severity of penalties that returned escapees might suffer' and 'the severity of conditions' in the re-education camps.[34]

Thus, in addition to the paperwork on the eight applicants mentioned above, Rizzo and Goodwin-Gill also carried with them to Canberra the latest information on conditions inside Vietnam and on people displaced in the region. The Sydney Branch Office had sourced the details from UNHCR Headquarters in Geneva and the Regional Office in Bangkok, and compiled them into a briefing paper. The document set out how those people escaping Vietnam by boat would likely face serious political difficulties if returned to their country, and were generally of a race, ethnicity or social group that authorities in Vietnam were targeting, or were of a political persuasion 'hostile to that of the current ruling class'.[35] Moreover, there was information that those Vietnamese who had voluntarily returned to their country had since been imprisoned, and had not yet been released.[36]

This briefing paper had been circulated to committee members before the meeting. After Rizzo and Goodwin-Gill were driven by Commonwealth car to the Department of Immigration and Ethnic Affairs' new offices in the suburb of Belconnen, senior Immigration officer Norman Hoffmann and another staff member involved with the DORS procedure greeted them, flipped through the evidence once more and said they 'thought it would be sufficient to persuade the DORS Committee to start making some positive determinations'.[37]

Once assembled in a conference room, the meeting began with introductions between Goodwin-Gill and committee members from the four government departments. As Goodwin-Gill recorded it, the discussion proceeded as follows:

> Nearly 1¼ hours was spent by the committee in an exercise of heart and soul searching. The topics discussed included: conditions in the SRV; the lack of information about what actually happened in that country; the notion of persecution; whether politico/economic measures of general application could amount to persecution; the inadequacy of interview reports.[38]

Rizzo and Goodwin-Gill soon realised that if the UNHCR briefing paper had been read, 'it had certainly not been digested'. They had to give reports of instances in which people who had been returned were shot, or where red marks had been placed above the doors of houses belonging to ethnic Chinese. They explained that a person sent to a 're-education camp' by the Vietnamese authorities could endure indefinite detention, hard labour and little food, and if released could be forcibly placed in a 'New Economic Zone' and have their business or other private property nationalised.[39] The two men spent the meeting stressing 'time and again' that detailed information for each case was hard to come by 'and that in any event it was not essential to the determination of refugee status':

> It was emphasised that a refugee was essentially someone who did not enjoy the protection of his government [...] enough was known about what was happening in SRV to justify the finding that most of the cases came within Article 1 of the 1951 Convention.[40]

Afterwards, Goodwin-Gill wrote in his notes that 'the Committee did not appear to be greatly moved by these arguments'.[41] Nonetheless, seven cases were recommended for refugee status, the eighth for compassionate/humanitarian leave to remain.

At the next meeting, on 3 November 1978, the debate began again. This time members gathered to consider the cases of fourteen Vietnamese: some applicants were Catholic, others were merchants or known anti-Communists; a few were associated with escape organisers, or were the younger relatives of Vietnamese who had already been assessed. According to the official DORS minutes stored in an Australian government archival record, the Foreign Affairs representative, a Mr Scott, told the room that he had seen 'very little evidence' that applicants had a genuine fear of return. Goodwin-Gill asked, 'Have you spoken to any of these people personally?'[42] The answer was no. As Goodwin-Gill then recorded in his own notes, the two proceeded to disagree on UNHCR's mandate and the evidentiary requirements of the DORS procedure:

> Mr Scott retorted that the Committee could not accept economic migrants within its definition of refugee, as UNHCR did. The Legal Adviser objected strongly, and stated that economic migrants were not to be found mentioned in the mandate of the Office.[43]

Both the official DORS minutes and the UNHCR record of this meeting can be found in the respective archival collections, and both clearly show a lengthy and heated debate over these fourteen cases. The Foreign Affairs representative was, in the UNHCR record of the meeting, 'most hostile', and essentially 'preferred to refuse refugee status on the basis that unobtainable evidence had not been obtained'.[44]

The archival records of DORS meetings are revealing, because there are clear and unexpected differences in the way that respective departments viewed the Vietnamese who had made their own way to Australia. The same individual did not necessarily represent each department at each meeting, but when voting patterns are observed over the years 1978 to 1983, the representatives from Foreign Affairs and Attorney-General's were far more likely to express a negative opinion on individual Vietnamese cases than their fellow committee members. The issue was largely about the nature of decision making, and whether particular applicants could be brought within the Convention definition of 'refugee'. Where Immigration, Prime Minister and Cabinet and UNHCR applied a flexible interpretation of the Convention, Foreign Affairs and Attorney-General's took a categorical approach.

On some occasions, it appears that the negative perceptions of the outflow that were colouring public debate in Australia had also filtered into the views of representatives from these two departments. They would occasionally go so far as to argue that some applicants were 'economic migrants and draft dodgers' who feared poor living standards.[45] Even after committee members had visited Darwin in April 1979 to meet people who had recently arrived, the Foreign Affairs representative stated that 'the Vietnamese of Chinese ethnic origin to whom he had spoken were not Convention refugees', 'they were simply capitalists looking for an opportunity to remain capitalists'.[46] 'The Chinese in Vietnam were not suffering discrimination, their life-style was simply being altered to bring them into the main-stream of Vietnamese life.'[47]

As noted in other chapters of this book, Foreign Affairs was invested in Australia's favourable image abroad, and in maintaining positive working relationships with its neighbours in the region. For these reasons, the department did not support turning boats back, but its representatives on DORS were not necessarily inclined to view those who sailed to Australia in overly positive terms. Indeed, one or two Foreign Affairs representatives took quite a cynical view of individual applicants' claims or, as Rizzo phrased it in a letter of complaint to that department, seemed 'to voice the most negative comments on applications that do not indicate unquestionable political persecution and/or punishment'.[48]

It is possible that the view of the Foreign Affairs representative was shaped by the briefing information on conditions in the SRV compiled by their department. Importantly, in the case of DORS debates over non-Vietnamese applicants during this period – people fleeing Syria, Iraq, Iran or Afghanistan (many of the same countries of origin for refugees today) – I have found evidence of a discrepancy between the content and timeliness of briefing information that Foreign Affairs brought to meetings as compared to that presented by UNHCR, and evidence that on occasion other DORS attendees felt there was 'a degree of bias or subjectivity' in Foreign Affairs briefing material.[49] Indeed, in the aforementioned comparative study in the *Stanford Journal of International Law* of 1983, Avery concluded that none of the ten countries he had studied, including Australia, had 'ensured that solidly competent, fully informed, and fundamentally impartial individuals conduct interviews, make decisions, and review determinations from the arrival of refugees at the border through final appeal'.[50] Whether the situation was similar with DORS' assessment of Vietnamese cases is not clear.

The minutes of DORS meetings do not record the way that each representative voted on every single application. However, a small number were recorded within the UNHCR files (which provide a more systematic record of DORS meetings than the Australian government archives) and thus while not a perfect measure by any means, they can be compiled and compared, showing distinct differences between departmental opinions: Foreign Affairs voted to recommend refugee status or compassionate/humanitarian leave to remain less than 40 per cent of the time; Attorney-General's was lower, at less than 25 per cent of the time. In contrast, on more than 70 per cent of the occasions on which the representative from Prime Minister and Cabinet is recorded as expressing their opinion on a case, they voted to recommend refugee status or compassionate/humanitarian leave to remain. When faced with the arguments of Foreign Affairs and Attorney-General's representatives, the representative from Prime Minister and Cabinet would usually side with Immigration to make a positive recommendation.

The voting patterns of the Prime Minister and Cabinet representative on DORS align with the preferred answer in Fraser's 'say yes, say no' choice. In his memoir, Fraser refers to a Cabinet submission by the Minister for Immigration in November 1978, in which MacKellar had lamented that limited information and resources meant 'our capacity to test the stories of refugees is limited', and that government therefore couldn't say with confidence 'that every Vietnamese who presents himself is a refugee'.[51] As Fraser and his co-author Margaret Simons noted, one of the Prime Minister's advisers had annotated a copy of MacKellar's cabinet submission to point out that it was equally impossible to tell if boat arrivals weren't refugees.[52]

The most interesting story within the archival records of DORS is about the Department of Immigration and Ethnic Affairs. MacKellar might have promoted a guarded image to the public, but when it came to assessing individual boat arrivals' claims, Immigration was leaning towards 'yes'. The department's representatives voted to recommend refugee or compassionate/humanitarian leave to remain for Vietnamese boat arrivals more than 80 per cent of the time.[53]

And within committee debates, Immigration would often endorse UNHCR's expert opinion; on occasion they would both remind the other Committee members that if Vietnamese people had spent time in a refugee camp in Malaysia or Thailand before sailing to Australia, this was irrelevant to their claim for Australia's protection.[54] Where Foreign Affairs or Attorney-General's would question the relevance of an applicant having spent time in a New Economic Zone, the Immigration representative would refer Committee members to UNHCR publications, which made reference to 'victims of general economic measures', and the UNHCR representative would advocate 'the view of a minority being forcibly obliged to abandon its traditional way of life, in the commercial, cultural and linguistic sense'.[55]

That Vietnamese 'boat people' were allowed to remain in Australia has been well acknowledged in the existing literature, from academic studies to personal accounts. Indeed, those fleeing Vietnam at that time were generally regarded by the United States and UNHCR and others as refugees. It is therefore little surprise that they were granted permanent stay in Australia. But the decision making on individual refugee claims has long been a mystery. By working through the available UNHCR minutes, and counting the 921 decisions that were made on the boat cases (these have to be counted as decisions rather than as individual applicants due to the nature of the archival records), it becomes clear that boat arrivals had a very high approval rate, at over 80 per cent, for either refugee status or compassionate/humanitarian leave to remain. The committee postponed cases on 154 occasions, and only 19 recommendations were for rejection.

What did rejection mean, exactly? In the case of the Vietnamese, it did not mean deportation. In fact, it appears that rejected applications were not sent on to the Minister, but were instead referred back to the committee for reconsideration. Goodwin-Gill became aware of this on 3 November 1978, after his second DORS meeting, when he had a conversation with Ian Simington, the Head of the Department of Immigration's Refugee Branch at the time:

> Mr Ian Simington indicated to me informally that a policy existed whereunder no boat person's application for status was to be refused or to be allowed on purely humanitarian grounds. For this reason the Department of Immigration would continue to have any potentially negative cases deferred ('for further inquiries') and reconsidered time and again.[56]

Just over two weeks later, at another DORS meeting on 22 November, Hoffmann opaquely explained the policy. The Attorney-General's representative, Peter Byrne, asked the Immigration Chair, 'Why has no Indochinese been refused?' He received the following in reply:

Mr Hoffmann replied: 'Because of public
commitments. Because of government decisions that
only (genuine) refugees will be allowed to remain; all
those rejected will be liable to deportation.'[57]

At the end of that year Goodwin-Gill wrote the following in
his report to UNHCR:

The Committee is aware that, under existing
government policy, no Indochinese application is to be
rejected. It has also found that, where it rejects such an
application but nevertheless recommends asylum on
humanitarian or compassionate grounds, the case will
be referred back to the Committee to enquire further
and reach a positive decision.[58]

The debate between committee members over Vietnamese cases was rigorous – both the UNHCR and Australian
government minutes of meetings show this very clearly
– but the fact that the Immigration department leaned
toward 'yes' caused particular tension. And after Hoffmann
obliquely explained the Department of Immigration's position to committee members on 22 November 1978, there
ensued months of debate and frustration over the assessment process.

By early 1979 the committee had a backlog of around
500 applications, the vast majority of them Vietnamese boat

arrivals.[59] Hoffmann admitted to Goodwin-Gill in January 1979 that 'he felt the Committee was fed up with being pushed to accept weak cases'.[60] Some departmental representatives became more vocal in their criticism; the representative from the Attorney-General's Department complained that 'the Committee was bending too far to bring applicants within Article 1 of the Convention'.[61] But Immigration pointed the finger in the opposite direction, arguing that 'the criteria invoked by the Committee' appeared 'to have varied with every meeting', and it was concerned for cases which should have been approved for refugee status rather than compassionate/humanitarian leave to remain.[62] For its part, UNHCR was of the view that the decision making process had become too restrictive through the Minister for Immigration's emphasis on 'genuine' refugees, and the Legal Adviser argued that the committee should be more willing to recommend compassionate/humanitarian leave to remain instead.[63]

At one lengthy meeting on 15 March 1979, debate raged over a number of Vietnamese applicants and matters came to a head. The Foreign Affairs representative favoured rejection '*pour encourager les autres*', a warning to others, 'to kill the idea that all those arriving directly in Australia are accepted'.[64] In reply, the Immigration representative made 'a very strong plea' for at least a recommendation of compassionate/humanitarian leave to remain over outright rejection; the department had evidently relaxed its insistence on a recommendation for refugee status, and now believed 'that humanitarian treatment should be accorded to all those who left SRV under present conditions'.[65]

At the next meeting, on 21 March, the Committee voted to reject another three cases, and in response the Immigration representative John Forster warned members that if they did not at least make a recommendation for compassionate/ humanitarian leave to remain, this might mean the applicants concerned could be returned to Vietnam.[66] He 'stressed the seriousness' of the recommendation to reject, and asked: 'How could the Minister for Immigration avoid a situation where the Committee had agreed that the applicant before them was not worthy of humanitarian consideration?'[67]

Even Immigration did not know the answer to this question; it turns out that at this point, 'no Indochinese rejections had yet been passed to the Minister and the form of any such recommendation had not therefore been decided'.[68] After Forster had spoken, Goodwin-Gill told the Committee that if rejections were indeed passed on to the Minister, UNHCR would make its own representations directly to him.[69]

The committee debates on non-Indochinese asylum seekers are a very different story. Individuals from more than forty-six other countries around the world – men and women from El Salvador, Ethiopia and Turkey (to name just a few) – submitted applications for refugee status at this time, and the departmental representatives made assessments as varied as the claims, personal circumstances and countries of origin of the applicants. The Department of Immigration and Ethnic Affairs was certainly not leaning toward 'yes' in every case. In fact, when the same small quantitative exercise is repeated for DORS decisions on non-Indochinese applicants, Immigration's votes accord quite closely with those of Foreign Affairs, and are in favour of refugee status or compassionate/humanitarian leave to remain around 45 per cent of the time (only slightly more often than they voted for rejection).[70] Attorney-General's votes remain roughly the same, while Prime Minister and Cabinet stands out as being in favour of refugee status or compassionate/humanitarian leave to remain on almost 70 per cent of occasions, more often than any other member of the committee.

The style of debate on non-Indochinese applicants is demonstrated by the Committee's consideration of the case of a Kurdish applicant from Iraq in May 1980. The meeting was chaired by Ian Simington, and there was a great deal of conjecture over the validity of this applicant's fear of persecution and the credibility of his story. The representatives from Foreign Affairs and Immigration suspected that this applicant's expressed motivations for migrating were spurious. One remarked 'that the government was determined "to get rid of" the present applicant' because he was 'demonstrably trying to get round the Migration Act'.[71]

The representatives from Prime Minister and Cabinet and Attorney-General's shared the reservations about the man's credibility but, as Goodwin-Gill recorded in his notes, were prepared to give the benefit of the doubt. Ultimately, the case was deferred for further investigation, but after such a lengthy and fruitless debate, the Attorney-General's representative, Geoffrey Dabb, couldn't help but note that 'had the applicant been Indochinese, the Committee would have accepted him'.[72]

The question of whether Vietnamese boat arrivals should be processed through individual, case-by-case determination under DORS had been clarified in those planning sessions of 1977, but with a backlog and frequent reconsideration of cases, it was revived in committee debates in 1979. Attorney-General's wanted individual assessment but thought that in theory, if the Minister for Immigration could 'bring in' refugees selected by 'his officials' in South-East Asia, 'then he would seem also to be free to declare that direct arrivals also qualified as refugees'.[73] Foreign Affairs had worried that group determination might set an unwanted precedent. There could be 'grave dangers', the representative Keith Baker mused during one DORS meeting in March 1979, that 'a blanket recommendation' might 'encourage a shipload of four or five thousand to turn up in Darwin in the expectation that finally all would be allowed to remain'.[74] But individual determinations were time consuming and resource intensive, and Foreign Affairs soon came to pressure Immigration to process the Vietnamese cases differently to those of normal asylum seekers.[75]

For well over a year Immigration defended its insistence on individual assessment – to allow group determination of boat arrival cases would mean reneging on public commitments to rigorously process and accept only 'genuine' refugees. Boats were expected to keep arriving, and thus, Forster told his fellow committee members, if the government was to reassure the Australian community that its reception of asylum seekers was rigorous and controlled, 'it was unlikely that Cabinet would agree to any general statement classifying direct arrivals as refugees'.[76] As debate continued through late 1979 and well into 1980, the representative sympathised with fellow committee members: he would have liked to 'write out' the entire caseload too, but this would be 'politically impossible'.[77] Another senior Immigration official, who had worked processing refugees from camps in the region, chastised Foreign Affairs and Attorney-General's for their persistence on the issue: 'it would be unacceptable', he argued, for any government to essentially enable a group of people to resettle in Australia 'simply by coming here'.[78]

Ultimately, it was an Immigration initiative that changed the Committee's workload: in December 1980, after 823 Vietnamese had been granted refugee or humanitarian/compassionate leave to remain, a further 241 people whose cases had not yet been resolved were referred to an alternative 'regularisation of status' program set up that year by Immigration Minister Macphee, designed to give amnesty to people living within Australia without formal residency status.[79] The very small number of Vietnamese who sailed to Australia after this point appear to have been assessed once again through the DORS process.

Whether any of the decisions to reject Vietnamese applicants were passed on to the Minister, and those individuals ultimately removed from Australia, has not been conclusively disproved, but it would appear from both the UNHCR and Australian government archival records that those who sailed to Australia from Vietnam and applied for protection were allowed to remain. In departmental files the majority of those listed as 'rejected' were recorded as having been subsequently approved for stay on humanitarian grounds.[80] A few were recorded as being resettled in countries to which they had stronger ties.[81] At a lengthy DORS procedural review of July 1980, after more than 90 per cent of applications from boat arrivals had been considered, the senior Immigration staff chairing the meeting maintained the official government line: even though those who had sailed to Australia to seek asylum thus far had been granted protection, they said, this 'did not necessarily mean that all future cases would be' – this acknowledged the function of a status determination procedure, but was also a portent of things to come.[82]

3

A country of resettlement

'I present these as a challenge to our humanity,
knowing where we must come out!'

Lou Engledow, to Minister MacKellar, 1978

In late 1977, a team of twelve Australians checked into a
hotel on the east coast of Malaysia. They were part of the
'South-East Asia Special Mission', and comprised five officials from the Immigration Department, five interpreters, a
medical officer and an intelligence officer.[1] They were there
to interview Vietnamese refugees for possible resettlement in
Australia, and were instructed 'to intercept' and select those
'who would otherwise try to reach Australia' on their own.[2]
Another team, 'South-East Asia Phase Two', would succeed

this team and others still would follow. At Immigration's prompt, and to ensure Australia maintained its resettlement efforts, the US State Department also pledged that its staff would try to interview and select those who might otherwise attempt to sail directly to Australia.[3]

This was the strategy to 'stop the boats at source', and the Secretary of the Department of Immigration at the time, Lou Engledow, advised his Minister that it offered 'the most desirable and practical short-term solution'.[4] Immigration officers had already visited refugee camps in Thailand with a similar objective, to 'arrange a regular intake' – something that MacKellar publicly claimed would remove the need for risky boat journeys to Australia.[5]

Just over 970 men, women and children had already made the journey by this time, including in that one election campaign week of November 1977.[6] They had steered their small craft to Darwin, Port Keats, or the Cambridge Gulf in remote Western Australia, or were found drifting off Broome by Australian patrol vessels.[7] Some groups were reported to have written 'SOS Vietnamese Refugees' across the side of their boats, or painted 'Show me the way to Australia' on the roof.[8] Another group was said to have steered along the shoreline of Doctors Gully in Darwin, right past the house of a senior Immigration officer.[9]

The government's public emphasis on control of entry was one part of the story. Asserting it was another. At the end of 1977, UNHCR staff in Sydney reported back to headquarters in Geneva that the handful of refugee boats were raising 'questions of inadequate defences, fears of epidemics and of an invasion by cheap labour'.[10] In Darwin, residents told local MPs they could see boats passing by their front windows.[11] Some of the wooden or steel-hulled craft that successfully carried refugees to Australia also brought quarantine, health and narcotics concerns.[12] In the eyes of the Immigration department, accustomed to managing entry, the refugees were also considered to be creating 'a precedent for the bypassing of official procedures'.[13]

For these many reasons, the Fraser government wanted to 'halt or reduce' the movement of refugees sailing to Australia; the question was how.[14] 'The only way', MacKellar told me, 'was to process as many of the people before they came to Australia as we possibly could' and 'to play our part in the resettlement process, and get others to do it. And that's what happened'. In the end, this is (roughly) what happened, which is noteworthy, because I have found evidence that other options were aired and (in some cases) considered as a result of challenges along the way.

When the Special Mission arrived in Malaysia in late 1977, there were around 7000 Vietnamese who had put to sea and were now sheltering in coastal camps in Malaysia and Thailand (in addition to the many thousands who had struggled overland to Thailand).[15] UNHCR was involved in funding their care and maintenance, and UN agencies had sought to rehabilitate large numbers of internally displaced people in post-conflict Vietnam by providing emergency supplies and replacing agricultural equipment.[16] Through interviewing new arrivals at the Pulau Tengah camp, on an island off Mersing in Malaysia, Australian authorities had concluded that the exodus from the country would henceforth be steady but modest: around 1000 people were expected to depart from the ports of Southern Vietnam each month,[17] and roughly 350 of them would choose to press on south to Darwin. The SRV was known to be putting in exit controls which, in time, would make it harder for people to escape.[18] Fuel was becoming harder to buy or to stockpile.[19] Journalist Henry Kamm reported in the *New York Times* on 'an open campaign of intimidation' by the SRV, in which authorities broadcast announcements through the streets that 'traitors' to the revolution would be severely punished.[20]

Whether the architects of Australia's resettlement strategy believed it could really discourage boat journeys, or whether it relied on other factors affecting traffic into the Gulf of Thailand and through the Java and Timor seas, was unclear. Based on reports from Australia's Joint Intelligence Organisation, Immigration assessed that while escape was 'no mean feat' at present, 'it is at least safe to predict that it will not become any easier'.[21] Intelligence suggested that the numbers would, ultimately, 'steadily diminish'.[22]

An Immigration officer called Elaine Moloney was among those who set up desk space at the top of a local hotel in the Malaysian city of Kuantan, while her colleagues travelled back and forth along the coast interviewing refugees who sailed in and might sail out again. 'Everybody thought it would be a short-term movement', she said years later. Immigration started out believing that they could 'process them all, and then the job would be finished in a year'.[23]

In published histories of the exodus, 1978 is commonly seen as a turning point, because the predictions made early that year were soon disproved. The SRV intensified discrimination against ethnic Chinese residents and some religious minorities, while forcibly relocating students, merchants, former officials and others into 'New Economic Zones', and continuing the long-term detention of thousands in 're-education' camps.[24] Although the SRV had moved to appropriate fishing vessels and had increased surveillance on land and at sea, more and more people committed to the decision to flee, and the *Song Be 12* was not the only boat to be commandeered by desperate people. By May 1978 the number escaping the SRV each month had doubled, and soon after, ASEAN governments reportedly anticipated that the outflow would 'increase significantly beyond present levels'.[25] Fraser's cabinet was advised that the SRV was expropriating private property, and that Vietnamese were also suffering from a scarcity of food and would likely take enormous risks to escape.[26] The Ministers for Immigration and

Foreign Affairs were of the view that the Australian government faced 'some difficult decisions'.[27]

At around 5 p.m. on 17 March 1978, a steel-hulled fishing trawler, the *VNSG1028*, sailed out of the main port of Jakarta and onward to Darwin. Some of the 108 people on board had journeyed all the way from Saigon, and others had climbed aboard at the Pulau Tengah refugee camp in Malaysia due to their uncertainty over the wait for a resettlement place.[28] This boat was part-owned by the Vietnamese government, and when it arrived in Darwin speculation was rife that it had been hijacked.[29] With attention still on the fate of the *Song Be 12* and its crew, who were awaiting escort back to Vietnam, a small band of unionists gathered to protest as the passengers of the *VNSG1028* were bussed from the wharf. An official from the Vietnamese government Department of Transport, Nguyen An Son, who was in Darwin to arrange return of the *Song Be 12*, stood nearby and watched, telling the media that these refugees were 'pirates'.[30] As Norman Hoffmann concluded preliminary inquiries, and told journalists that the refugees' 'credentials' were in order (internal departmental documents reported that some had previously been approved by United States officials in Malaysia),[31] a further eleven vessels were reported to be en route via Indonesia, and twelve more were spotted moored near Pulau Tengah and deemed to be capable of sailing south. Engledow advised MacKellar that more than 700 people could be involved.[32]

The Minister asked his department to prepare 'a paper on the possible options for dealing with unauthorised boat arrivals in Darwin'.[33] The incoming head of the Immigration department's Refugee and Special Programs Branch was Ian Simington, who would occasionally chair DORS, and he put together a list for Secretary Engledow. On 28 April, the Secretary drafted up the list to send to the Minister, explaining that while 'not in order of significance', 'it logically reduces the options in a way that I must agree with'.

I came across this list quite recently while browsing files at the National Archives in Canberra. It reveals some now-familiar thinking. The options were:

Put any suspected hijackers on trial.

Send any suspected hijackers (captain and crew) back to Vietnam under escort without trial.

Reprovision and refuel all boats, tow them beyond the three-mile limit and encourage them to find some other country to land in.

Rigorously (and probably arbitrarily) separate genuine refugees from the others, and send the others back by plane, either to Indonesia, Malaysia, Thailand or Vietnam.

Tell the Governments of Thailand, Malaysia, Singapore and Indonesia that we will put the entry of their nationals (including students) on to a quota and for every refugee that enters, one is dropped off the quota.

Tell the Malaysian and Thai Governments that our continuing contribution to UNHCR funds, for expenditure in their regions, depends on them stopping refugee boats leaving their shores.

Do not allow any people to land from any boats which arrive in an Australian harbour, leaving them tied up indefinitely at some quarantine point until they get tired and sail away.

Treat boat refugees almost as lepers, segregating them into special camps and giving them minimal standards of support.

Construct a major holding centre in some very remote area to a standard of construction, maintenance and supportive care in no way different to the environment the boat people left in Malaysia or Thailand; hold them in such a camp indefinitely and dribble them into the regular hostels as circumstances permit.[34]

The seventh option, that refugees would simply 'get tired and sail away', was completely unrealistic, but the penultimate idea was something else. I have found evidence that a former leprosarium near Darwin was considered by some staff to be a potential holding facility in the event of a large influx of people.[35] The idea of 'minimal standards of support' reflected a discussion within the department as to the deterrent value of a reception facility on Australian territory, which I detail further in chapter 5.

In retirement, former Prime Minister Fraser told an interviewer that less palatable refugee policy ideas were in the papers of the Department of Immigration and Ethnic Affairs, and the above list tells us he was right.[36] In our interview, the former Prime Minister had offered the view that there was a 'narrow core' of people in Immigration who 'regarded themselves as gatekeepers' to Australia.[37] But as the suggestion to 'treat boat refugees almost as lepers' was not recommended by Engledow nor adopted by government, and neither were several other ideas proposed in this list, it also suggests that if there were some staff who 'regarded themselves as gatekeepers', then there were others who pushed back on these ideas, such as fellow senior staff in Immigration (including the Secretary) or the Minister. Perhaps other considerations (international law, diplomatic relations or domestic politics) took precedence.

There is a handwritten preamble to the options that reads: 'I present these as a challenge to our humanity knowing where we must come out!' I understand it to be Engledow's handwriting. The Secretary was known as a highly capable administrator.[38] Spelling out these extreme ideas is likely to have been an attempt to demonstrate just how limited the government's options really were. Indeed, Engledow closed by saying that the options in the list were all feasible, just 'highly unpalatable'. He cited the legal and political impediments:

> The pursuit of any course would bring us into conflict with some interest group, e.g. other Governments, international bodies, international opinions, local political opinion, local welfare groups and the media.[39]

Similarly, just four weeks earlier, Simington had been working within Prime Minister and Cabinet and had been briefed on the imminent arrival of the *VNSG1028*. He had duly prepared advice for the Prime Minister that deportations or turning boats around were 'not practical, legal or moral options'.[40] A month on, Simington may have still believed this and, like Engledow, chose to list the extreme options to underscore a preferred outcome. Simington was regarded by colleagues as a 'stormy individual'.[41] Perhaps the change of department – or the arrival of the *VNSG1028* and another boat that same week – provided licence for the blunt and strongly worded expression of other ideas.

The role of the department was to provide objective advice and to canvass all relevant options, a process described in another archival record from this era as 'putting all the options and implications they could think of even if only to knock them down'.[42] From this perspective, the items listed here are perhaps less surprising, despite their wording and various implications. As the number of people fleeing Vietnam, Laos and Cambodia increased through 1978 and 1979, these ideas would resurface again. Some, such as turning boats back, were implemented around this time by governments in the region, and then by the United States Coast Guard in response to Haitians seeking refuge from that country's dictatorship in the early 1980s.[43] At the United Nations General Assembly in 1984 the High Commissioner for Refugees drew attention to 'a perceptible tendency on the part of certain States to resort to measures of "deterrence"'.[44] In Australia, most of the proposed options never came to fruition during this period, although as I will discuss in the following chapters, two or three were given further thought.

Using resettlement to 'stop the boats at source' and discourage risky sea journeys was not straightforward. For one thing, Australia's resettlement commitments were initially halting and modest. MacKellar wrote to the Prime Minister in February 1978 to report that staff of the 'Special

Mission' needed to return home, and he requested support for an ongoing Immigration presence in Malaysia as well as funding to increase the transfer of refugees to Australia.[45] The government announced an additional quota of 2000 people the following month, but further places were soon required.[46] The task of accessing, interviewing and selecting people was a tough one for Immigration officials and the medical officers and intelligence staff with whom they liaised. There is a photo in the department's annual report of 1979 showing officer Steve Carter at one of the island camps east of Malaysia, pen in hand, sitting across a table from his interviewees, with a crowd of attentive waiting families watching on. At night Carter stayed in the camp and slept on the table.[47]

The efficiency of resettlement also relied on other states. Reports back to Canberra in late 1977 and early 1978 indicated that Australian officers could select people for transfer to Kuala Lumpur and have them on a Qantas flight within weeks, whereas procedures followed by the United States could take months. 'And in the meantime', Australian intelligence agencies reported, 'we have evidence' that some refugees tire of the wait for a place in the United States and 'sail here in small boats'.[48]

So, in April 1978, while Simington and Engledow were sketching out that list of options, a delegation of senior Immigration officials flew to Washington to hold talks with Under Secretary of State for Political Affairs David Newsom and Shepard C Lowman of the State Department's Office of Refugee and Migration Affairs, as well as representatives from the National Security Council, the Immigration and Naturalisation Service, and the House and Senate Subcommittee on Immigration, Refugees and International Law. Derek Volker and colleagues made the journey not only to discuss the selection of 'boat cases' from the camps, but also to emphasise the difficulties Australia faced as small boats continued to land in Darwin. The visit was part of what one Australian newspaper called 'a complex, partly secret diplomatic effort' to 'exploit' Australia's 'special relationship' with the United States, based on their shared strategic interests.[49] Each country wanted the other to increase its resettlement intake, and both wanted to 'internationalise' the issue so as to distribute responsibility more widely for resettling those who had been displaced. President Jimmy Carter's administration had pledged an additional few thousand places for Indochinese refugees, but had faced opposition within Congress to a larger intake.[50] Caught between community advocacy for more resettlement and heated complaints about hijackings and 'rackets', the Australians needed United States support to ensure that those who'd made landfall in the region would not set out to sea once more.

Herein lay a particular challenge to the 'stop the boats' strategy: refugees did not necessarily brave the journey south of their own volition. At various times during the long years of the Vietnamese exodus, authorities in some host countries undertook their own efforts to discourage people from landing. Not long after the fall of Saigon, Singapore shut its harbour to new arrivals unless there was a guarantee that they would be resettled abroad.[51] Later, Singapore set a 90-day time limit and decreed that it would host a maximum 1000 people at any one time, and although reluctant to allow commercial vessels to disembark people rescued at sea, did establish the small 'Hawkins Road' refugee camp, which operated from 1978 to the mid-1990s.[52]

In Thailand, official attitudes hardened as the years went on and the number of people seeking refuge increased. Having provided refuge to more than 160 000 Laotian, Cambodian and Vietnamese boat and land refugees since 1975, with numerous camps for each group scattered along the eastern part of the country, by 1978 (if not earlier) authorities under the government of General Kriangsak Chamanan began preventing boats from landing, and infamously pushed back thousands of Cambodian refugees sheltering in the mountainous border region in June 1979.[53] Speaking at a conference in Canberra a month later, the Thai ambassador to Australia, Wichet Suthayak-hom, warned there was no need to ask the Thai government to show humanity, because it had been overwhelmed by humanity.[54] In his speech to the same audience, the UNHCR Legal Adviser, Dr Goodwin-Gill, critiqued a reluctance on the part of any state to honour first asylum: 'One can only ask', he said, 'what price humanity?'[55]

In Malaysia, the official response by Prime Minister Hussein Onn's government to several thousand boat refugees in 1976 through 1977 was inconsistent, and permission to land and remain temporarily was said to depend on a range of factors, including the assistance of external organisations, the nature of media coverage, or the simple timing of arrivals.[56] Reports back to Canberra emphasised the impressive generosity of the Malaysians, and in particular the efficiency of the Malaysian Red Crescent Society.[57] The Society was closely involved in rescuing people at sea and working with UNHCR to provide care for the displaced, and it received UNHCR's highest honour – the Nansen Medal – in 1977.[58] At a ceremony in Geneva, High Commissioner Prince Sadruddin Aga Khan praised 'the profoundly humane attitude' of the Society and its thousands of volunteers. By this stage, he said, Malaysia was hosting 3700 people:

> […] crammed in tiny craft, men and women, old
> people and children, having just enough food and
> water to last a few days, face the perils of the high seas
> and often drift from one port of call to another on
> a journey, the end of which may never be in sight: –
> losing their last glimmer of hope when the master of a
> passing ship turns a deaf ear to their calls. [59]

The Society and other non-governmental organisations would continue their work as operational partners of

UNHCR, but public opinion complicated the Malaysian response to the boats. Australian authorities understood that countries of first asylum could encourage (or were encouraging) people to sail south not only because resettlement was not keeping pace with the influx of refugees, but also because in some areas local residents – including rural farming or fishing communities – resented the increasing number of arrivals, partly because of the impact they had on local resources, and partly on account of a 'traditional enmity' toward ethnic Chinese or Vietnamese.[60]

In 1978 Malaysian authorities, as well as those in Indonesia, were believed to be towing seaworthy vessels out to sea, but the fate of the refugees turned back is unknown. Word arrived to Immigration that there existed 'an efficient system' of 'free repairs, maintenance, provisioning and the necessary navigational aids' in both countries, and each boat was said to be pointed in the direction of Australia.[61] Mac-Kellar advised Cabinet throughout 1978 that hardening attitudes in the region would leave Australia as the ultimate destination.[62]

Under Prime Minister Hussein and President Suharto respectively, Malaysia and Indonesia made it public in 1979 that they would turn boats away in the absence of further resettlement guarantees.[63] Horrific stories emerged of refugees drowning as their boats were towed out at speed by Malaysian naval patrol vessels, breaking into pieces in the waves.[64] If they did stay afloat, men, women and children risked starvation, storms, or, increasingly into the 1980s, vicious robbery and rape by Thai pirates.[65]

At Volker's meetings in Washington in 1978, Immigration and the State Department agreed that it was necessary to guarantee to countries in the region that they would resettle refugees in return for allowing the boats to land in those countries.[66] But could local authorities in Malaysia, Thailand, Singapore and Indonesia also be pressed to 'seize, impound or immobilise boats'?[67] The two sides agreed that they could make joint approaches to regional host countries on this subject, and United States and Australian staff in the region liaised more closely on these initiatives.[68] Through efforts to 'dissuade or prevent refugees from coming to Australia without prior authority', the resettlement program for these same people could continue apace.[69] United States officials were said to be 'surprisingly forthcoming' in regard to the idea:

> They suggested that this should be raised with the Governments concerned and that unofficial action might be taken in some circumstances, as far as possible with the cooperation of the local authorities (especially in Malaysia) to immobilise vessels.[70]

It is not clear whether or how Australia and the United States made these approaches to local authorities or carried them out. Years later, a former Immigration official called

Greg Humphries would tell the ABC that the Australians had personally drilled holes in boats, and the anecdote was repeated in print for an edited collection of Chief Migration Officers' memories. Citing quarantine concerns, Humphries recalled that he and others sought to immobilise the boats and capitalise on the fact that local Malaysian authorities were only allowing refugees to land if their boats were unseaworthy.[71]

While I have found no further evidence for this kind of 'immobilising' activity on the part of Australian Immigration officials, they were clearly motivated to keep people in countries of first asylum awaiting safe transfer to Australia, the United States or elsewhere. For Immigration officers at the scene, this was no doubt based on the human suffering they witnessed. Some were said to have been in tears while debriefing their superiors in Canberra, and other former Immigration staff have spoken movingly about clambering aboard fishing trawlers or large ships that had reached the shores of Malaysia or Hong Kong, opening the hatch and seeing hundreds of desperate children, women and men crammed on top of one another in the hull below.[72] 'The feeling I had', Wayne Gibbons has recalled, 'was one of absolute horror and despair'.[73] In urging Cabinet to put resettlement operations on a permanent, expanded and well-resourced footing, MacKellar explained that Immigration officers based in the region were 'grossly overworked' and 'under extreme pressure'.[74]

In July 1978, a helicopter flew close to the Thai-Cambodian border and hovered in view of the Laem Sing refugee camp. This patch of makeshift shelters on a sandy crop of Thai territory was a temporary home to several thousand people.[75] Among those who alighted from the helicopter were Immigration Minister MacKellar and journalist Keith Finlay, reporting for the *Australian Women's Weekly*. The Minister walked through the camp and spoke with refugees about how they had organised their escapes, and Finlay duly reported that 'their answers were consistent and no evidence of rackets was unearthed'.[76] Indeed, his resultant article gently emphasised an 'enormous incentive to get out', profiling five elderly men, 'each with one leg', who had told the Minister how they had escaped by swimming across a river at night.

Since Volker had met with State Department officials in Washington three months earlier, in April 1978, several boats had made landfall in northern Australia and Immigration anticipated many more to be on the way. Thus the Minister and his senior staff travelled not only to see the camps for themselves, but to attempt to convince host countries that Australia would assure resettlement if they agreed to 'hold the boats'. Engledow had previously thought there was little hope for this plan, based on the fact that he saw 'absolutely no advantage' for the host countries themselves, but that July the Minister made approaches to governments in Malaysia, Thailand, Singapore and Indonesia.[77]

Boats did not arrive in Australia for the next four months. When thirty-eight people made it to Darwin aboard a wooden-hulled vessel in November 1978, after having reportedly sailed within Indonesian waters for almost two months, they were the 46th group to land in Australia and one of the last.[78] At the end of 1978, Goodwin-Gill reported back to the UNHCR that MacKellar's 'entente cordiale' had been 'temporarily successful' in stemming the flow of boats to Australia,[79] and the Minister himself told Cabinet that the arrangements were delicate, and that Australia needed to commit to an increased intake because it was 'naïve' to suppose that countries of first asylum would be 'sympathetic to the Australian objective of having refugees held, perhaps indefinitely [...] until final settlement can be arranged around the world'.[80]

In *The Long Journey*, Nancy Viviani would later write that over the long term, the Minister's 'boat-holding' agreements had been successful, and both MacKellar and Fraser cited them as an example of good faith negotiation between Australia and countries of first asylum.[81] In the moment, however, it is safe to say that the outcome was less certain; displacement increased faster than resettlement commitments and the willingness of Malaysia, Indonesia and others to allow refugees to land and to remain temporarily had to be secured again over time, as the nature of the exodus changed in unexpected ways.

Through the second half of 1978 the international community became aware that the SRV was encouraging and profiting from the flight of its own people. No longer cracking down on 'traitors' trying to desert the regime, Vietnamese authorities instead were suspected of pushing ethnic Chinese and other oppressed groups to leave and to pay government agents a substantial sum along the way. The fee bought escape from persecution aboard refugees' own vessels or on larger vessels which were 'flying some flag of convenience'.[82] Alongside this development, opportunists in the region began to commercialise boat journeys, piloting rusting freighters such as the *Southern Cross*, the *Hai Hong*, *Tung An*, the *Huey Fong* and *Skyluck* to rendezvous with smaller craft off the coast of Vietnam and cramming thousands of men, women and children aboard, before trying to offload them on islands in Indonesia, the Philippines or in Hong Kong.

The UNHCR affirmed that if passengers paid to escape, this did not alter their claims for protection, and the agency eventually organised for those who suffered the journey on these ships to disembark or be resettled (sometimes after protracted negotiations – the *Skyluck* was forced to wait at sea for five months).[83] But once the provenance of the journeys became known, the Fraser government was reluctant to contribute to the resettlement of those on board, and coverage in the Australian press was equally critical of the SRV's involvement. In a meeting with UNHCR about the *Hai*

Hong, Simington argued that Australia could not respond to this ship by providing resettlement places, as Canada and the United States had.[84] Geographically, Australia 'was in a more difficult position than those two countries', Simington tried to claim, because as a destination for boat refugees, 'Australia found itself faced with a potential wave of 500 000 Vietnamese of Chinese origin still living in Vietnam'.[85]

The SRV's connivance shifted the already complex dynamics of this refugee situation. Hong Kong authorities established a clandestine investigations team to track large commercial vessels stopping at ports throughout the region, and began criminal proceedings against captains and crews. Meanwhile, ASEAN states resented the idea that Vietnam might be exporting its own population.[86] The commercialisation of flight forced the Carter administration in the United States to unexpectedly re-examine its predictions for the refugee outflow. Further south, US Ambassador to Australia Philip H Alston Jnr cabled back to Washington to warn that the Australians were feeling self-deceived.[87] Having committed to 'boat-holding' arrangements, MacKellar now submitted to Cabinet that Australia could not be seen to tolerate the SRV's actions, because in his view this would give 'the green light' for a large-scale migration that was not of the Australian government's design, but rather 'to a timetable and scale devised by another government and businessman'.[88]

The idea that the SRV was encouraging escape would come to preoccupy the international community for many months to come. This was a vexed issue that relied on multiple parties and broader strategic interests. Whereas host countries in the region were pushing back out to sea shiploads of dehydrated and weakened children, women and men, Australia's Foreign Minister Andrew Peacock was concerned that as an underpopulated 'white' nation, Australia would be 'especially vulnerable to international criticism' if it 'failed to respond in a humane manner to the arrival of boat refugees from Asia'.[89] Within the Department of Immigration and Ethnic Affairs, there was a genuine concern that a large number of people could sail into Australia's territorial waters. The government could not rely on 'established friendships', as MacKellar put it, to pave the way in international negotiations, nor could it rely on public statements by other countries; instead, both departments viewed Australia as being geographically and politically isolated.[90]

Through Australia's membership of the UNHCR Executive Committee, it had helped to push for an international conference in Geneva that December 1978 to address changes in the nature of flight and the need for global resettlement places. On the first day of the conference MacKellar took the podium and cited concerns that the SRV was encouraging flight, as the SRV's delegate at the meeting, Ambasssador to France Vo Van Sung, looked on.[91] Behind the scenes in Canberra, Australian officials had asked United States diplomats whether further alienating the Soviet-supported SRV was less acceptable than acquiescing to the way it was treating the Vietnamese people; the Australians argued the SRV's actions were 'humanly unacceptable, and increasingly politically unacceptable as well'.[92] When Australia's Office of National Assessments confirmed 'firm evidence' of SRV encouragement and the commercialisation of escape on 16 November 1978, the situation was described as 'a new ball-game'.[93] From this point, Ambassador Alston told Washington of a change in the Australian government's thinking at the 'sub-ministerial' level.[94] And for a few weeks toward the end of 1978 and into 1979, some ideas from that list of April 1978 were raised once more.

4

A country of 'first asylum'

'[W]e will not risk taking action against genuine refugees just to get a message across. This would be an utterly inhuman course of action.'[1]

Minister for Immigration and Ethnic Affairs,
Minister for Foreign Affairs, 1977

Since at least 1977 the Minister for Immigration had publicly rejected calls to force people out to sea. In the heat of that year's election campaign, MacKellar had jointly stated with Peacock that 'this government will not indiscriminately "make examples" of boat refugees by turning some of them back'. The two ministers clarified that the government's interest lay in preventing 'the entry of people falsely posing as refugees'.

The statement quoted above reflected a burgeoning emphasis on the rigour of existing procedures, underscored by the establishment of the DORS Committee. Then in mid-1978, after the Minister for Immigration had met men, women and children in camps across the region and secured 'boat-holding' arrangements with the countries that were hosting them, he had alerted his Australian audiences to the fact that boats could not simply be sent away without human or political consequences:

> We cannot afford to take a rigid stance. Simple
> solutions such as 'turn away all the boats', on
> examination, prove not to be acceptable. Turn away to
> where? To sink? To Malaysia? Why should Malaysia,
> with its crowded camps, accept back refugees who have
> decided to go to Australia?[2]

The Ministers for Immigration and Foreign Affairs may not have been the only MPs to face calls from members of the public to 'blow [refugees] out of the water' (as Mac-Kellar had described it), because the issue had to be clarified for Cabinet colleagues as well. In a joint submission in May 1978, the two advised Cabinet that turning boats around was unfeasible, due to the 'obvious political and international difficulties'.[3] It is likely these difficulties included Australia's ability to encourage host states within the region to hold boats, and its relationship with the United States. Several weeks before that Cabinet submission, at Immigration's meetings in Washington, the State Department had expressed alarm at rumours that the Australians 'might be preparing' to turn boats away; the United States, they said, 'did not see this as being consistent with the requirements of the UN Convention and Protocol'.[4] Australian Immigration staff nonetheless believed that the absence of turn-backs and other harsh measures had been noted by regional governments, by refugees in camps and by 'intended escapees' in Vietnam.[5] Late in 1978 with the advent of large commercial ships carrying refugees led by the *Hai Hong*, the department revisited an option that had been rejected publicly and at the Cabinet table earlier in the year, and rejected it once more.

In the middle of a DORS Committee meeting on 3 November 1978, the telephone rang; a coastal freighter carrying thousands of people was sailing in Indonesian waters and 'might well land in Australia'.[6] This vessel was reportedly overcrowded, with well over 2500 people.[7] As the UNHCR and governments around the world were soon to discover, the *Hai Hong* was part of the new commercial traffic in human lives. The Foreign Affairs representative who answered the phone, Mr Scott, took the default position that in this case, they 'could not be real refugees', and

Dr Goodwin-Gill had to remind everyone in the room that 'the fact that money had been paid or assistance given could not by itself negate a claim to refugee status'.[8]

Ian Simington was chairing this particular meeting and had heard rumours days earlier of the ship's existence. 'If this was an organised departure', he wrote to Secretary Engledow, 'the boat's arrival in Darwin would present us with a very useful opportunity to establish a precedent' – drawing international attention to Australia's policy of only allowing those found to be refugees to stay, or, he suggested, perhaps going further, and threatening to send people back to Vietnam (an action that, if fulfilled, could constitute *refoulement*).[9] Given the constraints on this latter course of action, it would appear that returning people to Vietnam would be an empty threat.

Indonesia refused entry to the *Hai Hong*, and the Malaysian government refused to allow passengers to disembark without resettlement guarantees.[10] For days, requests to resettle those onboard were cabled to and fro between the United States, UNHCR, France, Malaysia, Australia and others, while the freighter sat in limbo off the coast of Malaysia. Cables from Australian missions in the region suggested that the *Hai Hong* could head for Darwin. As mentioned in the previous chapter, Simington had met with the UNHCR Regional Representative in Australia, Gilberto Rizzo, on 14 November to try to defend Australia's reluctance to contribute to resettling the refugees onboard.

The UNHCR ultimately secured places for the refugees in Canada, West Germany, France and the United States by early December.[11]

The UNHCR's Regional Representative in Kuala Lumpur, Rajagopalam Sampatkumar, had issued a statement on 3 November expressing some apprehension about the motives of the owners, agents and captain of the vessel, which MacKellar echoed in his own press release three days later.[12] But once Sampatkumar had boarded the ship a week later and spoken with the stranded passengers, his impression and message shifted. And as the possibility of more shiploads became reality over these weeks, the UN High Commissioner for Refugees himself, Poul Hartling, sought to actively dispel any notion that refugees on large vessels were any different from those on tiny craft. There should have been no confusion, he told a gathering of states in Geneva on 11 December, as to the humanitarian problem that the *Hai Hong* represented, because 'if it were not the concern of the international community, then of whose concern was it?'[13]

Simington had carefully mentioned to Rizzo that Immigration and Foreign Affairs had discussed 'the possibility of turning the *Hai Hong* back to the high seas', and 'expressed the hope that this would not happen', without revealing that the idea had by now been firmly ruled out, once again.[14] Simington went on to explain that if the SRV authorities were indeed supporting the exodus of their population, then in his opinion it would only be encouraged to continue in this endeavour 'if Australia did not take a "tough" attitude', a point that his minister made to Cabinet later that month.[15] In Simington's argument, Immigration officials had had to consider how to 'make an example' of the *Hai Hong* in order to 'get a message across'.[16]

Had the *Hai Hong* made it to Darwin, the Australian government would not have had the legal authority to tow the freighter out to sea. This was made clear following an inter-departmental meeting on 9 November 1978, when staff from Immigration, Foreign Affairs, Attorney-General's, Defence and Transport had set out the possible courses of action under domestic law and international treaties, dependent on the *Hai Hong*'s proximity to Australian territory.[17] Intercepting the freighter on the high seas was deemed to be 'very dubious in law and clearly to be avoided'. And while the Australian Navy 'may be able to fire a shot across its bows', staff at the meeting also considered this legally problematic. It is not clear from the archival record whether this last suggestion came from Defence or another department, but the Foreign Affairs representative left the meeting with a curt reminder that his or her department would 'be most unhappy if the Navy put a shot across the bows of any vessel'.[18]

Notwithstanding a lack of legal authority, there was surely another impediment to turning the freighter around. Not only had the US State Department already indicated that it disapproved of the idea of turning back boats, but the United States and Canada were publicly emphasising how important it was for states in the region to allow asylum seekers to land, and both encouraged support for this in international fora. Australia relied on states in the region allowing refugees to land, as the basis of boat-holding arrangements. Could Australia seriously consider a unilateral course of action if a ship was on the horizon and there was 'evidence of trafficking'?[19] In January 1979, an interdepartmental committee reported on the possible responses to 'a large group whose bona fides were dubious'.[20]

This committee was known as the Taskforce on Refugees from Indochina; it was chaired by Immigration and included representatives from Foreign Affairs, Prime Minister and Cabinet, and the Office of National Assessments (ONA), an agency that had been established by Fraser to co-ordinate and consolidate the analysis of intelligence.[21] In the process of compiling its report, Foreign Affairs also consulted with UNHCR. Then, two weeks before the submission went to Cabinet, Norman Hoffmann, who was privy to the Taskforce, took Goodwin-Gill aside to make something clear:

> [...] despite recent ministerial statements on the subject of Indochinese refugees, it should not be supposed that Australia was intending to welch on any of its international obligations.[22]

Goodwin-Gill replied that UNHCR had 'naturally taken that for granted, but it was reassuring to hear'. Hoffmann had been closely involved in establishing the Refugee Branch within the Department of Immigration and Ethnic Affairs, had experience interviewing refugees as they landed in Darwin, and was accustomed to working closely with the UNHCR.[23] One wonders why Hoffmann felt the need to offer this reassurance. He was likely referring to MacKellar having made statements about 'departees', but Hoffmann may also have had in mind the wide-ranging ideas that the Taskforce was working through at that very time.

On 23 January, the Taskforce report went to Cabinet. It presented a sequence of steps that the government could implement if a large vessel suspected of trafficking arrived:

First step – Bluff – A firm public statement that Australia will not accept the people concerned; efforts to contact master of vessel to ensure warning is understood.

Second step – To intercept and try to physically turn away vessel at 3 mile limit.

Third step – In the event of vessel arriving at an Australian port to hold it at a remote location, under guard with instructions to leave forthwith; this position should be maintained as long as possible.

Fourth step – If forced to land people, a transit camp in a remote locality and with secure containment should be used and it should be made clear that persons concerned would be required to leave Australia; efforts should be made to persuade country of origin to accept people back (except for any recognised subsequently as refugees). This position should be maintained as long as possible.

Fifth step – If compelled to yield on step 4, persons would be granted refugee status, accepted as refugees but not granted resettlement in Australia; efforts should be made to secure their acceptance for resettlement elsewhere.

Sixth step – Failing the fifth step Australia would have to grant resettlement.[24]

The Department of Prime Minister and Cabinet advised that the sequence overlooked 'the political reality' that if the first step – a 'bluff' – failed, the government would have little alternative but to move to the sixth step and accept those onboard.[25]

I have cited these six steps here not only to note their similarity with Australian asylum policies in recent years, but also to reflect on the intention of their authors. The purpose of the document was to lay out all the options, no matter how unworkable they might be (something the Task-force readily admitted).

Some steps sound familiar to the options that Siming-ton and Engledow had raised the previous year. Holding people at sea until they left of their own accord remained just as unrealistic. How long could that last? Where would this 'remote location' be? It would require authorities, in the Taskforce's view, to 'tough it out'; the report recognised this could not be sustained indefinitely, particularly in the event of a stalemate, although as an initial recourse the Taskforce deemed this preferable to 'the precedent of giving in'.

Looking at the sequence as a whole, one can see the points at which later Australian governments, under prime ministers Howard, Rudd, Gillard, Abbott and Turnbull, diverted from the final outcome of resettling refugees in Australia. Howard played out the 'bluff' with the MV *Tampa* in 2001, as David Marr and Marian Wilkinson expertly detailed in their book, *Dark Victory*, followed by the second, third and fourth steps.[26] On that occasion, how-ever, the Howard government was 'toughing it out' against Captain Arne Rinnan, the master of a ship who had rescued 438 people from drowning in the Indian Ocean.

The second step – intercepting and turning people back – was implemented in 2002 as Operation Relex under Howard, and again under Abbott's Operation Sovereign Borders (that time with almost no exceptions). The Turn-bull government has continued a practice of placing asylum seekers on state-of-the-art lifeboats and setting them adrift in the direction of Indonesia, or handing them directly back to the governments from which they have fled (such as those in Sri Lanka or Vietnam).

The Taskforce noted that if a boat was in distress (whether deliberately immobilised by those on board or not), Australian authorities would be obliged to rescue and assume responsibility for the survivors. It did not detail a variety of other practical (and humane) considerations involved in turning away a refugee boat. It is not clear how or whether these issues were thought through. What if a passenger had been sick, or pregnant? Would Australia reprovision boats with fuel, food and water? Where else would they sail to? Cabinet agreed on 23 January 1979 that the steps needed further examination.[27]

The fourth step became policy under the Keating government when it introduced mandatory detention (a subject I examine in the following chapters). The remote locations were within Australia, but moved offshore in the early 2000s when Howard opened detention facilities in Nauru and Papua New Guinea. Suspended in 2008, the Gillard government reopened the facilities in 2012 and they have been maintained under successive Labor and Liberal governments.

The fifth step, in which 'efforts should be made to secure [refugees] acceptance for resettlement elsewhere', is close to where government policy stands today. Note the wording here implies flexibility ('efforts should be made'), and the sixth step provided for resettlement in Australia should these efforts not work out. That was because although the Taskforce proposed that Australia could potentially give refugees first asylum but resettle them elsewhere, it acknowledged that other states were unlikely to accept refugees held in Australia, given Australia's small population and history of immigration.[28] When, in 2013, Rudd announced that refugees who arrived by boat would never be eligible for resettlement in Australia, he removed that flexibility once and for all. Robert Manne has described this as 'absolutism' within immigration policy and the Immigration department's organisational culture.[29] It has led to a situation in which the Australian government negotiated controversial resettlement deals with Cambodia in 2014 and the United States in 2016, and has left 2000 people held offshore waiting several years for a durable solution, unable to reunite with children or partners in Australia.

In preparing its report the Taskforce had expressed a vain hope that the nation's international efforts and resettlement program should work to eliminate requests for asylum in the first place. But in leaning toward the sixth step (resettlement), while still planning for a hypothetical ship, the Taskforce noted that as a signatory to the Refugee Convention and Protocol, and as 'a humane government respecting human rights', Australia had a commitment to provide 'sanctuary to genuine refugees within its territory', and had an obligation 'not to forcibly return those genuine refugees to the country from which they have fled'.[30]

It is worth looking closely at this reference to Australia's obligations under the Refugee Convention. The wording above sets out two commitments: the obligation not to send individuals back to a place where they may fear persecution (the principle of *non-refoulement* under Article 33(1) of the Convention), and the need to provide 'sanctuary' within Australian territory to those found to be refugees. As Mary Crock and her co-author Kate Bones observed in 2015, in recent years Australian government asylum seeker policies have reflected a 'selective reading' of the Convention, in which the principle of *non-refoulement* is seen as the only requirement for states parties.[31] In comparison, the second commitment above implies that the protection Australia affords to refugees must go further than this fundamental provision, to encompass the full range of rights and protections under the Convention (such as the rights to education, to access courts, to work and to obtain travel documents) as a comprehensive expression of Australia's obligations under international refugee law.[32]

A large ship carrying thousands of people did not arrive (and never has). It is therefore impossible to know for sure exactly how the Fraser government would have responded if that hypothetical vessel had materialised. It is fair to surmise that it would not have taken steps one to five because by mid-1979, it had approved an alternative plan. Because

the Taskforce recognised that international law did not con-
done turning boats back to sea, and noted that the government wanted to manage passengers of a hypothetical large
vessel in a way that did not breach the Refugee Convention,
a subsequent Cabinet submission thus recommended that
'on humanitarian grounds and for reasons primarily flowing
from our obligations under the Convention', the government should not take action against passengers aside from
assessing their claims to be refugees.[33] It considered impos-
ing sanctions on the master, crew and others responsible
for the vessel to be the best approach; Cabinet agreed to
proposed legislation to impose penalties on those involved
in 'bringing people to Australia without prior authority, particularly for profit',[34] and the Immigration (Unauthorised
Arrivals) Bill 1980 was drafted.[35] The files show that some
staff within Immigration doubted whether a large vessel
was still a possibility at this point, six months after the *Hai
Hong*, but MacKellar was 'insistent' that the submission on
the draft legislation be put to Cabinet.[36]

It is important to note that during this period, mid-
1979, the Labor Party was also working through its own
set of potential policy responses to the boats. At the Party's
National Conference in July that year, the Opposition's
spokesperson on Immigration at the time, Dr Moss Cass,
recounted the varied and extreme suggestions that had been
put forward: these included sending 'a gunboat out' to shoot
the boats out of the water – 'then they would stop coming'.

Cass explained to the Labor audience members why this
course of action was unfeasible:

> [...] it was quite clear we could not tow them out
> to sea. You could imagine the reaction – send a boat
> out to sea. Where will it go after getting all the way
> to Australia – or will it just drop anchor and sit there
> [?] You can imagine when I said to [the journalists]
> when I was pushed on this issue [...] they always are
> asking about 'What will you do when a boat arrives off
> Darwin with 3000 people?'

> '[If we] send it out to sea [...] what do you think will
> happen?' [Journalists] will then all charter boats or,
> better still, helicopters [...] will fly around [...] taking
> dramatic photographs of people suffering [...] You can
> imagine the impression on the Australian community.[37]

The fact that this was a subject worth mentioning at the
Labor Party's major gathering indicates, along with the Australian government archival records, that there were many
within politics, government and the community, who had
to be encouraged to think through the consequences of
turning back a boat carrying vulnerable people.

On occasion UNHCR gained insight into these debates
within the Immigration department, and the agency's inclusion on the DORS Committee provided regular opportu-

nities to informally liaise with Immigration staff. After 248 people successfully reached Darwin in April 1979, the largest number for well over a year (and some of the last to arrive), Engledow drafted another set of options for the minister. A copy of this document was locked in a safe in Simington's office, and Hoffmann chaired the Refugee Branch while Simington was overseas. According to the UNHCR files, after a DORS meeting on 9 May Hoffmann took the opportunity to unlock the safe, remove the document and show it to Goodwin-Gill. His actions, and the document itself, hint at disagreement within Immigration over how to manage the continuing arrival of small boats and the potential arrival of larger ships.

The Secretary had written that from what he had heard, the claims of boat arrivals to be refugees were weak: they were 'not genuine refugees' but rather 'adventurous youths', 'spontaneous migrants' and others who did not wish to experience poor living standards in Vietnam.[38] He asked that 'urgent' and 'serious' consideration be given to returning future boat refugees to Vietnam, and reasoned that any political fallout could be offset by 'an announcement of an increase in the quota for refugees from camps'.[39] It was around this time that Immigration was preparing arguments for increasing Australia's resettlement intake, in the lead-up to ASEAN talks in Jakarta and a series of other international meetings, and thus the Secretary may have thought it an opportune moment to take a harder line closer to home.

As they looked over the document, Hoffmann confided that some senior members of the department, including Secretary Engledow, were 'hard' in relation to the boats, others 'in-between'.[40] It is almost impossible to assess his reasons for making these statements. Goodwin-Gill's notes of the conversation do not comment or speculate on Hoffmann's relationship with colleagues, but merely record what was said. The Minister, according to Hoffmann, was 'open to persuasion'.[41] And the Secretary's proposal was trying to do just that, as Goodwin-Gill set out in his notes:

> On the arrival of the next boatload of weak cases,
> it was suggested, the Department of Foreign Affairs
> should be requested to call upon the Vietnamese
> embassy to document those arriving for repatriation to
> Vietnam. The writer noted that such a practice would
> cost much less than keeping them in Australia, though
> he admitted that the national and international cost
> was 'not calculable'.[42]

The Secretary was referring to 'weak cases', and his suggestion should be read in light of debates within the DORS Committee about applicants whose claims did not fit the Refugee Convention definition. By this stage, April 1979, the Committee had voted to reject no more than a handful of cases, and UNHCR had supported some of these recommendations. But Goodwin-Gill had also advised that these applicants should be allowed to remain on humanitarian or compassionate grounds, 'account being taken of existing conditions in Vietnam and the likelihood of severe punishment for illegal exit'.[43] Thus, the 'repatriation' that the Secretary referred to may have meant involuntary return. It is not clear whether the Secretary intended that arrivals would have their claims formally assessed under the government's status determination procedure, or whether he meant Immigration officials should assume those with perceived 'weak cases' were not genuine refugees; the latter would be troubling, especially as under this proposal, Australia would arrange returns directly with the government from which the individuals had fled, and potentially breach of Australia's obligations under international law.

Perhaps, as Engledow had written atop the list of April the previous year, he had presented the ideas 'as a challenge to our humanity, knowing where we must come out!' Or perhaps an apparent 'hard' position on the boats was not enough to persuade MacKellar to take a radical course of action that would not only undermine Australia's 'boat-holding' strategy in the region, but also reverse the Minister's appeals to the Australian public not to forget the humanity of those coming by sea.[44] What is interesting about this document is that it suggests the Secretary was less willing to appreciate the need to grant asylum seekers humanitarian or compassionate leave to remain, in light of conditions for returnees in Vietnam. The Minister evidently did not share

(or at least did not act upon) the suggested position that
boat arrivals who did not fall under the Convention definition should be removed from Australia.[45] Certainly Engledow had acknowledged that the political costs of this action
were 'not calculable'.

Whether Foreign Affairs would have supported the plan
to 'call upon' the Vietnamese authorities, as Engledow suggested, and enjoin them to participate in the forced return
of Vietnamese is doubtful. Foreign Minister Peacock had
set out in Cabinet Memorandum 380 of 11 July 1979 that
Australia could not return people to a communist state.[46]
The fact that he did so indicates the issue required clarifica-
tion. In this memorandum Peacock also set out the foreign
policy implications of turning boats around, suggesting a
continued interest in this point as well. Perhaps, as stated
earlier, other MPs were facing calls from vocal members
of the public to take a restrictive approach to the entry of
Vietnamese refugees arriving by boat, but to do this, the
Foreign Minister argued, 'would court international pariah
status', and Australia would lose its international credibility
on human rights issues and its claim to have moved on from
the era of racially discriminatory entry policy.[47] Moreover,
pleas to 'hold the boats' would be untenable, he argued:
'given that we have lectured ASEAN countries about their
responsibilities as countries of first asylum, we would be
open to charges of hypocrisy'.[48] In an archival file dated
later that year, Gervase Coles indicated a reluctance on the

part of Foreign Affairs to trouble or dismay the UNHCR. It was embarrassing, he recorded, to face recriminations from UNHCR when Australia's relations with that agency 'are of considerable importance to us'.[49]

In mid-1979, the UN Secretary-General Kurt Waldheim scheduled a major international conference in Geneva to address what he called a situation of 'crisis proportions'.[50] At a pre-conference meeting in the United States mission on 10 July, permanent representatives to the United Nations in Geneva talked over whether the event would address the political elements of the problem – namely, the role of the SRV in encouraging departures – and not just the humanitarian consequences (as Waldheim envisaged). The French saw no point in an event designed only to promote resettlement places, as it believed this would result in 'pull factors'. Canada took a middle line, and wanted to use the conference to press the point that 'countries should neither force their citizens out nor shut them in', but others were less confident.[51] The need to increase resettlement places while addressing the root causes of flight made for a complex agenda. The US Ambassador to the European Office of the United Nations in Geneva, William Vanden Heuvel, told the room that 'everyone would be losers [...] if the conference fell short of what the world expects'.[52]

In Australia's assessment the SRV was the central problem, having targeted particular ethnic and social groups and allegedly profited from their flight. By now this view had gained some traction elsewhere, too; the Carter administration in the United States had joined with other G7 governments in Europe, the UK and Japan to issue a statement calling on Vietnam, Laos and Cambodia to end the hardship and suffering of their populations, and for 'the immediate cessation of the disorderly outflow of refugees'.[53] But in the wake of an ASEAN meeting on Indochinese refugees two months before the conference in Geneva, Australia's Ambassador to the Philippines, Richard Woolcott, cabled Canberra to suggest that a sole emphasis on the SRV's role would be perceived by Australia's regional neighbours as a deliberate distraction from further resettlement commitments.[54] Cabinet was therefore advised by the ministers for Immigration and Foreign Affairs to increase Australia's acceptance to 14 000 refugees in 1979–80 because 'our voice in international forums will only be as strong as our actions'.[55] The number was a 'calculated risk'; taking fewer 'might turn international opinion against us and discourage ASEAN control efforts'.[56] It was certainly an increase on previous years, but it was less than the increase that editors of some Australian newspapers were calling for in the lead-up to Geneva.[57]

When the Geneva conference took place, in mid-1979, most of the more than 2000 boat refugees who successfully sailed to Australia during the Fraser era had made landfall, and only a small number were still to arrive. More significantly, more than one million people had been displaced from Vietnam, Laos and Cambodia, but only 200 000 had been resettled abroad. The fate of the remainder – and those who would follow them – lay in the competing interests of relevant resettlement states. The exodus was at its peak, and UNHCR was urging resettlement countries to consider increasing their quotas.[58] The French had accepted 50 000 people (second only to the United States), and now took the position that the bulk of resettlement should be within the Asia-Pacific region; in their view, the Indochinese were 'an Asian problem'.[59] The Malaysians and Thais disagreed with the French, for obvious reasons. The British had accepted fewer than 2000, and were casting about for states to take some of the 57 000 people sheltered in Hong Kong (Australia deferred, prioritising those refugees who were closer to home and potentially capable of sailing south).[60]

There were also calls for new contributions. Papua New Guinea was brought into the debate amid uncertainty over what would happen should boat refugees arrive there. Briefed by UNHCR in mid-1979, Prime Minister Michael Somare's government reportedly rejected the idea of resettling Indochinese refugees for fear of creating 'an ethnic minority' in a largely homogenous population, which it said would lead to 'immediate and long-term social problems'.[61] It is worth noting that a similar concern remains critically important today, almost forty years later, in UNHCR's assessment of the long-term viability of Australia's extra-territorial processing and settlement arrangements, under which refugees who sought protection in Australia are to be settled in Papua New Guinea.[62]

The Geneva conference was also tasked with securing anew the 'boat-holding' arrangements, which came apart as displacement escalated and host countries sought to emphasise the need to increase resettlement commitments. In the first six months of 1979, Malaysian authorities pushed out to sea more than 50000 refugees, while Indonesia duly noted more than 30000 new arrivals. It was, according to news reports, Malaysia's way of nudging their ASEAN peer to agree to host a UNHCR processing centre.[63]

In his detailed history of the Indochinese refugee situation, *The Refused*, Barry Wain writes that tensions grew between the ASEAN states of Thailand, Indonesia, Singapore, the Philippines and Malaysia over the way that rejecting refugees at the border of one state invariably moved them to seek refuge in another – but Wain argues these issues were concealed in favour of solidarity.[64] As a neighbour, not a member of ASEAN, Australia was in a different position, and a sense of Australia's isolation is evident within the archival records. Twelve months after MacKellar's face-to-face guarantees, when host countries were desperate for more resettlement guarantees and the exodus was at its height, officials in Suharto's government told Australian diplomats in Jakarta that ASEAN members were thinking about co-ordinating 'joint anti-refugee efforts'. '[I]t is no good', they confided, 'for Indonesia and Malaysia to turn refugees back if the only result is to aggravate problems in Thailand'.[65] When asked 'that the same consideration might be considered to apply to Australia', the Indonesians could only reply that 'they would try to turn the boats back towards the north'.[66]

Ultimately, the Geneva conference generated the desired commitments to first asylum and an increase in resettlement: more than 135 000 additional places were pledged, twice the existing number at the time.[67] The United States alone doubled its annual commitment, while in place of a resettlement quota, Japan pledged to cover around half the cost of UNHCR activities in the region.[68] Controversially, Vietnam committed to a six-month moratorium on departures, under which it would attempt to prevent people from leaving without authorisation.[69] It had signed a Memorandum of Understanding with the UNHCR that became known as the 'Orderly Departure Program' (ODP), under which select groups of people would be allowed to leave. The ODP was the first time UNHCR would work with a country of origin to pre-empt the cross-border movement of people.[70] In their book *Escape from Violence*, Aristide R Zolberg, Astri Suhrke and Sergio Aguayo note the problematic inclusions and exclusions of the ODP and its use by the SRV as a vehicle for 'getting rid of undesirable social groups', such as ethnic Chinese.[71] Australia would come to negotiate a bilateral arrangement with the SRV in 1982 to facilitate family reunion cases, and under this scheme tens of thousands of Vietnamese would be brought to Australia over the following decade.[72]

The pledges in Geneva – and the temporary drop in departures that resulted – did not resolve the displacement in Indochina. The situation continued to evolve as more Cambodian refugees moved into Thailand, while Australian government archival records indicate that throughout the early 1980s there was uncertainty over whether the SRV authorities had control over mass escapes.[73] The refugee situation was not expected to ease. Rather, as Foreign Affairs reported in 1982, the number of people escaping Vietnam by sea was expected to continue 'at present levels of 60 000 to 70 000 per year'.[74] In Canberra, more intrepid journeys south were anticipated, as inward cables reported that boats landing in Indonesia were intending to reach Australia.[75]

When Immigration Minister Macphee introduced the Immigration (Unauthorised Arrivals) Bill in May 1980, he said he hoped it would prove to be 'an effective deterrent' for people-smuggling operations by both air and sea.[76] According to the Minister, the legislation was not directed at the boat people themselves, but instead sought to curb exploitative 'rackets' capitalising on displacement and 'profiteering from human distress'.[77] Macphee had received bipartisan support for the legislation from his Shadow counterpart, Mick Young, although, as other scholars have pointed out, the Bill was not without its critics in the Parliament.[78] To offset public criticism the Bill contained provisions that enabled it to come into operation on a date yet to be proclaimed, and only to remain in force for twelve months unless extended by a resolution passed by both Houses of Parliament. Macphee told the Parliament that authorities had no reason to believe a large ship was on its way, 'but we cannot afford to assume' that there would be no further arrivals given 'the pattern of recent history'.[79]

In the end, the *Immigration (Unauthorised Arrivals) Act* was enacted to deal with 146 people who arrived in Darwin in October 1981 aboard the fishing vessel the *VT838*, claiming to be from Vietnam. Concerns about the provenance of the boat had been raised before it reached Australia's territorial waters, and Macphee had asked the Governor-General to proclaim the legislation. Those on board were eventually deported when it was confirmed that they were not, in fact, Indochinese refugees, but were from Taiwan and Hong Kong, and had flown to Bangkok and set sail from Songkhla on the southern Thai coast.[80] In his monthly report for December 1981, Goodwin-Gill described how the vessel 'was part of a highly-organised syndicate':[81]

> [The] evident Thai design and construction, as well
> as the good health and condition of those on board,
> had already aroused suspicion when the vessel stopped
> briefly at Pilau Bidong; subsequent inquiries confirmed

that the trip had been organised to circumvent the migration law through abuse of the asylum process.[82]

Macphee told Parliament that Immigration officials and the Australian Federal Police worked closely with the Royal Hong Kong Police to investigate passengers' credentials.[83] 'Intensive interviews' were conducted, which the *Canberra Times* described as 'interrogations', in which Immigration officials had to separate the women and children from the men, and fight 'a psychological battle' in the face of the asylum seekers' hunger strikes and suicide threats.[84] The UNHCR files indicate that the Sydney Branch Office was kept 'fully informed of all stages of the investigation' and 'found no reason to intervene'.[85]

At the end of December, Australia transported 127 of the *VT838* passengers on chartered flights to Taiwan and Hong Kong, holding the remainder for further investigation before ultimately deporting them.[86] The *Canberra Times* reported that Immigration officials 'had to go to considerable lengths about secrecy when removing the deportees to the airport' for fear 'there were going to be demonstrations and that we'd have to drag people kicking and screaming on to planes'. This would, they reasoned, be 'very difficult to explain to people'.[87] Macphee had previously told Parliament that the crew would be prosecuted under the *Immigration (Unauthorised Arrivals) Act*, but in the end, Goodwin-Gill's files indicate that 'the sanction of deportation was finally preferred'.[88] Goodwin-Gill's end-of-year report for 1981 suggests that the handling of the *VT838* passengers did not raise objections from the UNHCR, stating that there had been no instances that year of abusive detention of refugees or asylum seekers, and 'no interventions were necessary to prevent *refoulement* or expulsion'.[89]

Three decades later, in a submission to a 2011 parliamentary inquiry on Australia's detention network, the Department of Immigration and Citizenship described the *Immigration (Unauthorised Arrivals) Act* as 'arguably the antecedent' to legislation introduced in the early 1990s and 2000s to deal with asylum seekers who arrived by boat.[90] Macphee takes a more nuanced view of this. Under Article 31 of the Refugee Convention, asylum seekers should not be penalised for unlawful entry, and the 1980 Act was not designed to penalise people seeking asylum. The former Minister saw a further difference between this and later pieces of legislation, arguing the approach to people smuggling in 1981 was underpinned by the Fraser government's resettlement from the region of the very same refugees who were potentially subject to smuggling operations.[91]

Macphee made the argument in 1981, and maintains it today, that the passengers on the *VT838* 'were economic immigrants who were bypassing immigration processes [...]. Meanwhile there were genuine refugees in detention camps whom we had to process'.[92] This language certainly sounds like a distinction that is often made by government today – the notion that Australia's annual resettlement program justifies a strict approach to asylum seekers – but the situations are not comparable, because the 1980 legislation was enacted for individuals who were, as UNHCR noted above, seeking to 'abuse the asylum process'.

Macphee had visited the camps in the region several months before the *VT838* arrived, and had received evidence from Immigration officers, as well as from studies by a UNHCR delegation and a United States research team, that the profile of those who fled Vietnam, and their reasons for doing so, had changed as time went on. Not unlike some other resettlement countries in the early 1980s, Australia was looking to wind back its intake from the region. But the issue was vexed, and on 15 July 1981 Macphee wrote to Fraser to state that despite question marks over some percentage of the outflow, 'genuine' refugees would continue to flee Vietnam in coming years and 'there will be a need to maintain appropriate arrangements to protect the interests of such people'.[93] The needs were still great and the 'boat-holding' arrangements were still as relevant as ever:

> The alternatives to not accepting them are unthinkable:
> to unduly overcrowd the Malaysian camps, to have
> Malaysia 'shove the boats off' and have many people
> drown, or have the boats head straight to Darwin.[94]

The strategy, he advised the Prime Minister, was that Australia would 'privately assure' Malaysia and Thailand that it would maintain its refugee intake but avoid publicising this fact, in the hope of avoiding any perceived encouragement to people still within Vietnam.

According to legal scholar Arthur C Helton, toward the end of the 1980s an increase in displacement in Indochina meant that international resettlement efforts no longer kept pace with demand, and this led to hardening attitudes in host countries. This created a situation that undid the achievements of the Geneva Conference in 1979, which Helton wrote 'had brought a modicum of order' to the refugee situation, 'and a sense of purpose in the efficacy of available solutions'.[95] In 1989 countries of asylum and resettlement again gathered for an international conference under a 'Comprehensive Plan of Action' (CPA), which aimed to resolve the displacement in Vietnam through repatriation or resettlement, and involved case-by-case determination of those in countries of first asylum. The plan attracted some criticism from scholars and advocates for shortcomings in the way that refugee status determination procedures were implemented in respective countries, and the subsequent risk that people who needed protection could be sent back to Vietnam from camps in the region.[96] Many camps were not closed until well into the 1990s, and the last Vietnamese to be processed under the CPA were reportedly 'expelled' from a camp in Hong Kong in 2000.[97]

By the mid-1990s, Australia had resettled almost 150 000 Vietnamese with considerable success, but by that time asylum seekers from Indochina had begun to risk boat journeys to Australia once again. They included Vietnamese who feared repatriation under the CPA from camps in the region, such as Galang in Indonesia, or had been displaced a second time after originally seeking asylum in China.[98] I will discuss the way that the Hawke and Keating governments responded to their arrival in the final chapter of this book.

5

A relatively friendly affair

'The officer in charge of the Station and his
medical and other assistants show a high degree
of compassion, interest and preparedness to help
which are clearly of benefit to those arriving in a
new environment.'

Dr Guy S Goodwin-Gill, 1979

On a clear Friday morning in April 1979, the UNHCR
Legal Adviser, Dr Goodwin-Gill, looked over Darwin Harbour and saw a 20-metre wooden fishing boat bobbing in
the hot sun. The *VT241* had been guided in by HMAS *Assail*
as daylight broke, its engine sputtering, and some sixty men,
women and children were on the deck and in the wooden

hull, the youngest a tiny baby. They were ethnic Chinese, from in and around Saigon, and had fled the southern port city of Vung Tau in late March with no maps, sailing experience or crew, steering 'on a bearing of which they had been advised, in the hope that they would strike land'.[1] The group claimed they 'had no particular intention to reach Australia', but had been given further directions by a passing ship and by locals in Timor.[2] The final stage of their journey had been typical of those asylum seekers who had recently stepped ashore; they were reported drifting in the Timor Sea days earlier, spotted by surveillance aircraft, and met by a Royal Australian Navy patrol boat approximately 90 nautical miles from Darwin.

Goodwin-Gill was in town with other DORS Committee members to see first-hand the reception of boat arrivals. He spent several hours on board the *VT241*, meeting the passengers and observing the health checks and other initial assessments. From what he had observed, the interceptions at sea were a relatively friendly affair:

> Any urgent assistance will be rendered by the patrol
> boat crew and it is evident that rations are often shared
> and that crewmembers frequently donate cigarettes.[3]

Once secured at a quarantine buoy, boats were subject to quarantine and customs inspection to detect the presence of monkeys, rats, insects 'or other infestations' as well as any 'dutiable cargo'.[4] The *VT241* was found to be 'riddled with termites'. Health workers checked passengers for serious diseases and distributed anti-malaria pills. Passengers were also subject to an immigration check to determine how they had escaped, from where, and the route they had navigated at sea. Police and officials from the Australian Security Intelligence Organisation and the Department of Immigration and Ethnic Affairs stepped aboard and employed translators where necessary.[5]

Goodwin-Gill met with the Regional Director of Immigration and Ethnic Affairs, Les Liveris, who said that if Goodwin-Gill should 'find any problems in the administration or treatment of the Vietnamese' he should 'bring them to him'. Goodwin-Gill then toured the East Arm Quarantine Station, situated some 13 kilometres from the centre of Darwin and overlooking the harbour, to see the facilities in which new arrivals were usually placed. The facilities were old and worn, but 'clean and well kept', and hut accommodation for 150–160 people was complemented, when necessary, by the erection of tents on concrete bases.[6] His impressions of the Quarantine Station were favourable:

> I was greatly impressed by the efforts of those
> responsible to create and maintain a viable institution
> out of very little material [...] [and] the extent to
> which the services of the refugees themselves are called
> in aid. In some respects this is due to the shortage of

staff, but the consequence of allowing the refugees
to assist in the running of the Station, to do their
own cooking, and to keep the premises looking
good appears to be of psychological benefit after the
enforced inactivity of a long sea voyage.[7]

On the occasion of Goodwin-Gill's visit there were 188
Vietnamese asylum seekers held at the station, all of whom
had arrived at various times in the preceding two weeks. As
Goodwin-Gill reported back to UNHCR, they were free to
engage in recreational activities, and were able to cook meals
for themselves with fresh ingredients ('food is plentiful –
rice, eggs, chicken, beef, fresh vegetables and fruit, sugar and
coffee'). They could also make use of 'a fish trap [that] has
been constructed by the sea edge' to which they had free
access: 'trevally and mud crabs are an addition to their diet'.

Goodwin-Gill met with the two staff who ran the Quarantine Station, and reported on the efficiency and quality of
medical services there:

Each passenger is given a thorough medical check [...]
any serious cases of illness are transferred to the local
hospital [...] During my visit a young man who was
losing his sight was referred to a specialist in Darwin
within a matter of hours.[8]

He also recorded that staff at the Quarantine Station 'show a high degree of compassion, interest and preparedness to help which are clearly of benefit to those arriving in a new environment'. He observed that any disturbances or outbursts of 'group rivalry' amongst the asylum seekers 'have been handled quickly and sympathetically'.

The length of time asylum seekers stayed at the Quarantine Station depended on the individual case, but it appears to have been between five days and two weeks. While there, they had further interviews with Immigration officials, and were then granted temporary entry permits and moved to migrant hostels in major cities while their applications for refugee status were formally assessed.

As Vietnamese asylum seekers braved the sea journey south to Australia from 1976 to 1981, there were several occasions on which these decent reception procedures were cause for reflection by the Department of Immigration and Ethnic Affairs. Goodwin-Gill noted that Australian authorities hoped that immigration, quarantine and customs procedures could create an impression amongst asylum seekers that arrival did not automatically mean they could stay permanently. Goodwin-Gill observed the way that application procedures were explained to new arrivals:

> At all times the Australian authorities attempt to
> make clear to those arriving directly that a favourable
> decision on residence is not automatic, that every case

is to be considered on its individual merits and that
residence will depend upon the applicant qualifying as
a refugee under the 1951 Convention.[9]

That Friday in April 1979, Goodwin-Gill found that the
VT241 had been reprovisioned with food and water and
'left at the quarantine buoy for around 72 hours'. When he
stoutly questioned the delay, Goodwin-Gill received 'a very
strong reaction' from Ian Simington, who was in Darwin
with visiting DORS Committee members, and who claimed
Australia was being 'tough' in this regard. In the end passengers were transferred to the Quarantine Station outside of
town when (as Goodwin-Gill wryly concluded) 'the necessary period of retribution in Darwin harbour' had elapsed.[10]

Perhaps the Department of Immigration had greatest
cause to consider reception arrangements in April 1978
in Washington, when Derek Volker tried to explain to the
Americans that boats were stirring resentment in the Australian community. In so doing, he explained the procedures
for receiving asylum seekers in Darwin. In response, Shepard C Lowman and other US State Department officials
drew a conclusion they could never reach today, telling their
Immigration guests they were not convinced 'that Australia
really is seeking to deter unauthorised arrivals'.[11]

By contrast, ever since the Keating Labor government
implemented Australia's system of mandatory immigration
detention in the early 1990s, the policy has been a source

of great controversy on account of the psychological costs to some of the people held within it (including children) and the human rights violations that it may involve. The policy contravenes Australia's obligations under the International Covenant on Civil and Political Rights, and the Convention on the Rights of the Child.[12] Fraser was a vocal critic of mandatory detention; Macphee has abhorred it as 'barbed-wire imprisonment, continuing cruelty and expensive folly'.[13] There was 'no barbed wire, no camps' under Fraser's leadership, as the former prime minister himself said. But the idea of some kind of facility was put to Cabinet by MacKellar on more than one occasion and, importantly, for more than one reason.[14]

There are several strands to this story. The first is familiar, and involves the potential deterrent value of a closed remote detention facility. There was ambivalence about this idea within government; a deterrent would require a certain standard of negative treatment, and detaining refugees from Asia in this manner could have unfavourable symbolic and social consequences. Further, given the desperation of those fleeing, and the international resettlement effort, would a detention centre act to deter or to encourage risky boat journeys?

The second strand involves a national debate over the logistical difficulties that Australia would face were a possible large-scale arrival of refugees to actually occur. The meaning of 'large-scale' appears to have varied in internal documents, in some cases up to or above 100 000 people. MacKellar justified the discussion of facilities on the grounds of managing entry, because 'if the numbers got to a certain extent, how are we going to stop them from travelling all over the place?'[15]

The third strand is often overlooked, and involves an international discussion about locations in which to host large numbers of displaced people, where they could safely reside and be processed for settlement. Australia was considered by some (at home and abroad) as a potential location for such a facility.

Inherent in each strand of this story was the question of whether or not Australia would bear responsibility for settling refugees held in a facility on its territory. This was an area of great uncertainty, given the ongoing flight from Indochina and potential future displacement. There was a clear desire to prevent refugees from regarding Australia, as Foreign Minister Peacock put it, as 'an inevitable and natural destination' in the region.[16]

A proposal for some form of camp went to Cabinet in May 1978, soon after the arrival of the *VNSG1028* had led Simington and Engledow to sketch new ideas. In the weeks leading up to the Cabinet submission, Secretary Engledow had been unconvinced that a detention or reception facility was the real answer to Australia's policy challenges. At best,

he wrote, it would be a 'back-up' to the strategy of stopping boats through resettlement, to hold those refugees who
'escape the net' of processing efforts in the region. In this
scenario Australia would keep accepting those who arrived
by boat but would transfer passengers to a reception centre
'pending decisions on their future'.[17] But Engledow preferred sticking with just the resettlement strategy alone. And
he wrote that using a reception centre as the sole strategy
was 'the least attractive possibility in the short-term'.[18]

It is not clear how the costs, operation or lifespan of the
hypothetical facilities were assessed during these few weeks,
but no doubt staff had discussed the issues. Given what is
known today about the detrimental outcomes of immigration detention – especially the fact that it does not deter
refugees coming by sea nor provide any resolution to their
protection needs – Engledow's assessment of the long-term
consequences was realistic and perceptive:

> My difficulty is that the reception centre concept as
> such will not stop boat arrival nor will it produce in
> itself a final answer.[19]

And as he phrased it, a detention facility would require a
'philosophy of management' that meant it could only be 'a
last-ditch or long-term solution'.[20] It is not clear what the
Secretary meant by a 'philosophy' of management. Given
the nature of camps that were set up in Malaysia, the

Philippines, Hong Kong and elsewhere by this point in the first few months of 1978, it is possible he was referring to a number of considerations, including: the physical nature of the facility (whether it would be 'closed' or would allow movement into the community); whether it would be operated and funded by Australia or by UNHCR; and whether Australia would commit to resettling all those held within it.

In late April the Secretary had advised his Minister that while all the options compiled by Simington were unpalatable, 'a major holding camp' was the only one that was practicable – potentially as a deterrent, but also as a way of sharing the responsibility. Indeed, set out at the end of the list, the Secretary mused that this unwanted option could be framed as a long-term commitment to international efforts:

> A decision to build that camp would signal to the
> world that we saw the refugee problem as an ongoing
> one and would indicate that we intended to deal with
> it in much the same way that the Malays, the Thais, the
> Indonesians and, indeed, various European countries
> ever since World War II have dealt with it.[21]

At that very time, when Volker and his colleagues were meeting with their State Department counterparts in Washington, similar ideas were being discussed. The then head of the State Department's Office of Refugee Affairs, Shepard C Lowman proposed that the Australians continue resettling from the region but treat the inevitable few who sailed south in the same way as they were treated in countries of first asylum. This would mean (as the Australians recorded Lowman's statement), that on arrival individuals would be placed 'in a land camp in some remote locality with the bare necessities of life'.[22] Lowman is regarded as having championed Indochinese refugee resettlement by the Carter administration during these years, and so his suggestion here was likely underpinned by the United States government's belief that all those escaping from Vietnam must be resettled.[23] Indeed, in making the suggestion Lowman offered that the United States could resettle two-thirds of the people held within an Australian facility.[24] Although the United States was against the idea of turning boats around, it evidently considered that it would be acceptable and possible to deter refugees through a detention centre 'Down Under' – as long as Australia's own resettlement program didn't stop.

Following the meeting in Washington the Immigration delegation reported back to the department that the idea of camps 'has many unattractive aspects', but the time might have come to consider the unpalatable options – those 'which fall short of turning away boat people but make Australia a less attractive destination than it has been up to date'.[25] Days later, at the beginning of May 1978, the Ministers for Immigration and Foreign Affairs took to Cabinet a proposal to construct 'minimum facility reception centres' away from major cities, as a means of processing boat arrivals for resettlement in Australia or elsewhere.[26] They recognised that such plans would need to be handled 'sensitively'. Archival records show that Fraser's own department advised against a holding centre, believing that while it might have some deterrent effect, it would not completely prevent refugees from attempting the journey south, and the 'domestic and international reaction' to such a facility would be emotive and hostile.[27] Cabinet instead decided that Australia should see whether the United States could speed up its processing in the region, and should try making approaches to host countries to hold the boats.[28]

Lowman and others from the US State Department had advised the Australians that 'it was a mistake to give too favourable treatment to unauthorised arrivals [and] some disincentives were needed'.[29] They were referring to the quality of accommodation, social security, language classes and other services available to refugees arriving by boat. The Immigration delegation returned home from talks in Washington in April 1978 convinced that 'there was no logical basis' for giving boat arrivals the same benefits as other refugees (despite the principle of non-discrimination under Article 3 of the Refugee Convention).[30] This was around the same time that the term 'queue jumpers' surfaced in departmental language. In that Cabinet submission of May 1978, Immigration and Foreign Affairs had considered abolishing social security payments to the boat arrivals while their applications were being processed, as a way to lessen Australia's attractiveness as a country of first asylum. The Department of Prime Minister and Cabinet advised against it, for this would 'not have the slightest deterrent effect'.[31] Indeed, as KS Hutchings of the External Affairs Branch wrote, it would be 'widely regarded as a vindictive measure'.[32] A year later, Cabinet agreed to query reducing social security payments to boat arrivals, and the Attorney-General's Department duly advised that this would not be consistent with Australia's international obligations; although it had initiated the inquiry, Immigration ultimately concluded that reducing payments would not deter asylum seekers from coming to Australia.[33]

After returning from his meetings with ASEAN members in mid-1978, MacKellar recommended to Cabinet that Australia must continue assuring regional hosts that resettlement would continue, and must keep encouraging others to contribute to this. In the meantime, however, although refugees had temporarily ceased making the journey to Australia, the government must not become 'complacent'. 'It is by no means unlikely', the Minister argued, 'that thousands of refugees will attempt to reach Australia'. He proposed that the department undertake a study into 'possible sites' and operations of 'a refugee holding centre in Australia', to be completed by mid-October.[34] Engledow had reasoned that a preliminary study would be useful to determine the 'pros and cons' of the idea.[35] In response to the submission, the Acting Assistant Secretary of Prime Minister and Cabinet, AC Kevin, advised that his department held 'strong reservations' about the idea, believing a proposal would pose 'political problems'. Should other ministers support the proposal for a study, it must examine not only the practical and financial elements of the issue but the political and social implications as well.[36] Exactly what these implications were was not specified, but Cabinet agreed that 'low-key' contingency planning 'might be advanced'.[37]

On 13 November 1978, when the fate of the *Hai Hong* was still being resolved, Engledow wrote to the Minister to recommend that press statements should emphasise 'the fragility' of the boat-holding arrangements. With rumours that another five freighters were boarding refugees, 'I don't think we should be telling the public that everything is still holding pretty well'.[38] MacKellar's public statements certainly became more practical at this point, as he emphasised the logistical challenges of receiving large shiploads of people:

> We must face a possibility that large numbers of
> people might turn up repeatedly on crippled vessels,
> entering and refusing to leave Australian ports.
> Without documents, they are virtually stateless and

> not returnable. The question for national government
> is not simply how does one help some refugees, but
> how can one react to the possibility that a tide of so-
> called refugees could sweep in? How does one check
> their credentials?[39]

The Minister was attempting to create a distinction between those who had fled in fishing boats and those who had paid their way out on large vessels, and therefore prepare the public for the potential arrival of a ship, and flag the possibility that this large group could be managed differently. In January 1979 Goodwin-Gill reported to UNHCR that MacKellar was attempting to promote a new term, 'departees', to distinguish those who had fled with the complicity of the SRV authorities from earlier boat arrivals and those resettled out of camps in South-East Asia. This was around the same time that Hoffmann reassured the Legal Adviser that Australia would not 'welch' on its responsibilities despite the Minister's public statements. The UNHCR had to nonetheless publicly reiterate its position that 'regardless of the manner of their exit such people were of concern'.[40]

In Cabinet, MacKellar sought support for a review of policy options.[41] 'We are still not in a position to cope', he said, 'with the physical implications of a boat possibly carrying over 2000 refugees arriving in Darwin', particularly if the vessel was deliberately immobilised by those on board. The government could not simply prevent this scenario 'by saying we have no camp to put them in'. He asked that Cabinet agree to 'the general thinking' on a reception centre, which would enable confidential negotiations to begin with the Northern Territory government. The Department of Prime Minister and Cabinet described the proposal as premature, and opposed commencing discussions with the Northern Territory.[42]

Whether the Northern Territory government actually wanted to play host to any formal centre was another issue. When preparing for the possible arrival of the *Hai Hong*, federal authorities had discussed with their Territory counterparts whether passengers could be accommodated in the Quarantine Station or a school, plus '100 odd caravans' or canvas shelters.[43] Staff in Darwin advised Immigration that the Territory Chief Minister Paul Everingham might not be on board with the plans, and indeed the following month Everingham told the media that a camp should be established on the Australian protectorate of Christmas Island, to 'take the pressure off' Malaysia and discourage refugees from sailing further south.[44] He reiterated the suggestion in the Northern Territory Legislative Assembly the following year, at around the same time that MacKellar once again flagged to Cabinet that a 'detention centre in Darwin' could one day be required.[45]

The question of how the international community could receive, host and process for resettlement large numbers of refugees had been brought to the fore thanks to the *Hai Hong* and its ilk. The UNHCR-led conference on Indochinese refugees held in Geneva in December 1978 considered the idea of 'refugee processing centres' based within the region. According to the UN Secretary-General Kurt Waldheim, the proposed centres would ensure that displaced people could be processed for resettlement 'in an orderly way within a specific time scale'.[46] In the lead-up to this meeting, Mac-Kellar told Cabinet that there was still a 'strong possibility' that reception centres would be required in Australia. These proposed facilities would possibly function 'under United Nations supervision and at United Nations cost', the Minister said, a suggested arrangement likely intended to internationalise responsibility for those held within them.[47]

Although Prime Minister and Cabinet provided advice that a holding camp was 'most undesirable',[48] the proposed study went ahead, and was reported to Cabinet in Submission 2906 of January 1979. It concluded that Australia should 'be totally opposed to the establishment of an international holding centre on its territory'. No matter the financial support from UNHCR or elsewhere, other countries would never resettle refugees held in 'an affluent, lightly populated, migrant receiving country' in South-East Asia.[49] Establishing a reception centre for refugees would cement Australia's role as a destination for boat refugees. Staff in

Prime Minister and Cabinet agreed, and viewed a holding centre as 'a last resort, only to be contemplated after the capacity of existing facilities and other alternatives have been fully assessed'.[50]

The idea of hosting camps was equally unpopular abroad, and deflected by governments in Asia, Europe and North America. In a meeting at the United Kingdom's mission in Geneva the day before the July 1979 conference, Malaysia and Indonesia proposed that centres be established outside the region, perhaps in the United States, New Caledonia, Japan, China or Australia.[51] In response the United States claimed that such camps would be financially unsustainable and would violate the principle of habeas corpus – 'refugees could not be held in centres against their will'.[52] The French declined to host, in line with their belief the refugee situation was 'an Asian problem'. Engledow told other delegates that Australia could not host camps either, partly for financial reasons.[53]

By mid-1979 the governments of both the Philippines and Indonesia had confirmed that they would dedicate space to constructing reception centres, with capacity for 50 000 and 10 000 people respectively. The UN Secretary-General declared this to be 'a major breakthrough'.[54] Within the Australian government, MacKellar and Peacock submitted to Cabinet that the value of the Indonesian centre was 'questionable',[55] but nonetheless that Australia should support the plan due to 'the absolute need to be seen to care about the problems being faced by ASEAN' and 'being willing to share in the solutions'.[56] Meanwhile, Australian authorities reportedly sought to approach Indonesia to see whether refugees who reached Darwin could be transferred to a new UNHCR-run camp in that country on the basis that they would still be resettled in Australia, even though Prime Minister and Cabinet took the view that this plan was equally unrealistic.[57] Opened the following year, the Philippines Refugee Processing Centre was a 750-acre (300 ha) camp on the coast of the province of Bataan, 'a bustling city' that would stay open for over a decade and house 350 000 people over that time.[58] The Refugee Processing Centre at Galang Island, on the northern side of Indonesia near Singapore, operated until the mid-1990s.[59]

Australia ultimately avoided the international pressure to host a facility, but while the Geneva conference of July 1979 was getting underway and the future of the outflow remained uncertain, the establishment of 'reception centres' or 'transit camps' was mooted again at home. It appears that because the exodus from Vietnam was escalating, the contingency planning was now a question of preparedness as much, if not more than, any deterrent value. How likely was an influx of refugees? Some staff in Immigration and Prime

Minister and Cabinet thought 'the possibility of large boat arrivals in Australia was extremely remote' by now, while for others an estimate of 20 000 arrivals was 'a small number'.[60] A scenario in which 'we really get inundated' constituted more than 100 000 boat people.[61] In June 1979 the *Canberra Times* reported that 'normally cautious bureaucrats' believed that an estimate of 150 000 was 'quite reasonable'.[62]

The issue of detention facilities remained 'politically sensitive', as Prime Minister and Cabinet phrased it.[63] This was made clear in press coverage of the issue, in which 'concentration camp-type detention centres [...] [involving] people behind wire fences patrolled by guards' were viewed as the last of a 'very short list' of options for Australia, but one that might need to be adopted should boat refugees arrive in large numbers.[64] As Labor's Spokesperson for Immigration, Dr Moss Cass had been advocating for reception facilities since 1978, as a means of managing 'the increasing number of people' sailing to Australia.[65] In July 1979 Labor adopted camps as party policy at its national conference. Cass argued that the temporary refuge camps would enable Australia to care for 'uninvited refugees' on behalf of the UN, based on the idea that different countries would share the final resettlement of these individuals.[66]

The policy was contentious. Mick Young, who was then the Labor spokesman for employment and industrial relations, spoke against his own party on the issue, arguing that the unlikely resettlement of the refugees elsewhere meant that temporary refuge would invariably turn into 'permanent ghettoes':

> If we are to have those people in the hostels
> permanently, and have people encamp permanently in
> the hope that someone would take them off our hands,
> within a few years, I would think we would have the
> White Australia policy being written back into the
> platform of the Labor Party.[67]

An editorial in the *Sydney Morning Herald* argued that the policy was 'well-meaning' but impracticable, while the *Australian* declared it 'out of step with reality and at odds with public opinion'.[68] On news of Labor's policy choice, the newspaper argued that camps would institutionalise discrimination between the Vietnamese refugees who only reached camps in South-East Asia, and those who had the 'perseverance and courage' to sail all the way to Australia.[69]

The Minister for Immigration judged the public mood was largely opposed to camps or other holding facilities. In an interview with the *Sydney Morning Herald*, published on 20 July 1979 and timed to coincide with Labor's policy choice, MacKellar stated that the government had ruled out establishing such facilities for the present time.[70] But when asked what the government would do if a freighter carrying 3000 refugees landed off Darwin, the Minister avoided a definite answer: 'Let us wait until that eventuality occurs. We want to make sure that it doesn't happen'.[71]

This was the calm circumspection that served MacKellar well. He then told the journalist about the extent of the refugee situation, and stated there might have been up to one million ethnic Chinese still seeking to leave Vietnam.[72] What he didn't reveal was that on 10 July 1979 Cabinet had agreed that to continue 'discreet' contingency planning for a possible influx.[73] Prime Minister and Cabinet had not been consulted about the contingency planning, but endorsed 'discreet and adequate inter-departmental examination'.[74]

The way that MacKellar and former Prime Minister Fraser remembered the proposals for detention directly reflected the political sensitivity of camps or holding facilities at that time, and their recollections were no doubt impacted by the fact that detention centres had come to fruition since they left office, and have since proved an ongoing source of controversy. In our interview MacKellar stated that 'there are all sorts of stories' about how submissions for facilities went to Cabinet during his time as Minister, and the archival records 'give a false impression of that'.[75] He believed his department did the right thing in canvassing what he referred to as 'detention' centres, because they were addressing a logistical problem:

> I think that they quite properly put forward a range
> of options, one of which was detention centres if, you

know, the numbers got to a certain extent, how are we going to stop them from travelling all over the place?[76]

In comparison, Fraser attributed the idea of detention facilities to the White Australia mentality that he thought lingered within the Department of Immigration. The proposals to Cabinet were, in his words, 'racist barbarism'.[77] Fraser did not deliberate on the internal political reasons behind the proposals, but his former Minister for Immigration did. In MacKellar's recollection a Cabinet submission was a means of placating the more hardline members of the party:

> But you had to put forward the options. And if you
> didn't put forward the options then you had to take
> into account the reactions of your fellow Ministers.
> Say you didn't consider that option, some of the
> more hardliners would have said, 'oh we've got to do
> something about this, we just can't have them coming
> in willy nilly and going everywhere'.[78]

MacKellar has said that he did not support the idea of detention centres, but put it to Cabinet in the knowledge that Fraser would refuse it.[79] Both would say in their interviews with me that the Minister for Immigration didn't push the issue.[80] Once Cabinet had rejected the idea, MacKellar said, 'then it's been addressed'.[81] These claims would fit with what is known about the then prime minister's use of Cabinet as a consultative, exhaustive process. Patrick Weller wrote in his study *Malcolm Fraser PM* that Fraser saw Cabinet as a central part of government and used it strategically to 'maximise his own influence' and gain consensus:

> Under his leadership Cabinet met regularly and considered the critical issues. However it was also politically convenient: Fraser understood the value of collective action, the advantages of drawing his ministers into decisions and the strengths of Cabinet commitment.[82]

MacKellar mused that Fraser's support for accepting Vietnamese refugees meant that Ministers were reluctant to challenge his opposition to detention centres or other facilities.[83] Yet in our interview and in his memoirs the former Prime Minister presented a slightly confusing picture of the decisions that his government made. He stated that the proposals to Cabinet were rejected every time and he would not stand for the idea.[84] He said he ensured they were quickly dismissed:

> [...] the consideration they got in Cabinet would have taken no more than five minutes every time they came up.[85]

Margaret Simons wrote in *Malcolm Fraser: The political memoirs* that Cabinet considered 'suggestions' for centre locations, but that the idea did not reach the planning stage.[86] But as Mike Steketee has pointed out, the archival record indicates that the idea 'received more consideration than Fraser suggests'.[87] Cabinet approved contingency planning on 10 July 1979.

It is thanks to this planning that researchers can now see how the rationale for – and consequences of – a proposed facility were weighed up. An Inter-departmental Committee on the Treatment of Unauthorised Boat Arrivals put together Plans A, B and C for receiving refugees (and a 'Plan D' for non-refugees), based on consideration of Australia's Refugee Convention obligations and community opinion, along with the projected costs for a new reception system.[88]

'Plan A' was the status quo.[89] This involved an entry procedure that seems unsophisticated in comparison to the vast border control system the Australian government has in place today. It was based on 'constant aerial surveillance' by the Royal Australian Air Force and a commercial company to try to ensure that boats were detected and then escorted into harbour by a coastal patrol vessel. The quality of coastal surveillance had come under scrutiny, as the occasional boat would arrive undetected, and criticisms were levelled at the federal government by MPs and the press in the Northern Territory and Western Australia from late 1977 through to 1979.[90]

Plan B involved 'limited restraint in holding centres' to support quarantine, customs and health checks if the numbers of boat arrivals increased markedly. It appears that the concept of 'limited restraint' meant that asylum seekers could still move around the community, but could not move to alternative accommodation elsewhere. The cost of their accommodation would be deducted from their social security payments.

Plan C was the most significant option from today's perspective. It provided for the operation of detention centres, which would remove asylum seekers from the community and 'avoid any risk of unauthorised assimilation'. They could be detained for up to six months, during which their 'rights and duties' would be comparable to that of jailed prisoners. Plan C was deemed to be most relevant to an 'exceedingly large scale influx'.

The inter-departmental committee then spelt out the issues involved. Secretary Engledow had requested detailed advice on the legalities of each option from the Secretary of the Attorney-General's Department, Alan Neaves. In this request, Engledow noted that there had been no decision on any of the options, and that some of the options the committee had been considering 'may prove quite unacceptable to the government'.[91] The first question posed to the Attorney-General's Department was: 'Could the contingency plans be implemented without departing from Australia's obligations as a party to the Convention [...] If so, how?' The formal response from Secretary Neaves advised that Plan C would breach the Refugee Convention and neither Commonwealth law nor international law would allow rights to be limited to those of a prisoner in jail (noteworthy advice given the move to mandatory indefinite detention under the Keating government).[92] Even a large shipload of people could not justify implementing Plan C in a way that would accord with Australia's obligations under the Convention, and any restrictions on movement would need to be time-bound and proportionate.

From the inter-departmental committee's perspective, Plan C would also generate 'an even stronger reaction from civil rights groups and some elements of the community at large'. At the same time, should there be a mass influx of the sort canvassed under Plan C, this form of closed detention 'would attract support from other elements of the community'.

For now, the committee concluded that Plan A was the best option under both domestic and international law:

> [...] the present procedures for dealing with
> unauthorised boat arrivals are adequate, if expensive.
> They are consistent with Australia's international
> obligations and provide a mechanism which conforms
> with present domestic legislation for treating persons
> who arrive directly in Australia without prior
> authority.[93]

The committee went on to state that the status quo 'would be at risk' in the event of a large influx which was 'in excess of available facilities and in numbers considered by Government to be beyond our absorptive capacity'. Exactly what that capacity would be was not made clear, but the committee suggested that in the event of a large influx, 'temporary holding while international resettlement opportunities were sought would be required'.

Whether these international resettlement opportunities would materialise was another issue. As stated earlier, opponents of facilities claimed that other states were unlikely to resettle refugees held in Australia. There was a counter-argument to this, expressed in the newly adopted Labor policy, which held that such facilities were actually a means of lessening Australia's responsibilities in the event of a mass influx. If boat arrivals were secluded in camps or centres away from population centres, and had not become part of the Australian community, this would lessen their claim to stay in Australia. It was a similar line of reasoning to that used to support the establishment of remote detention centres under then Keating government Immigration Minister Gerry Hand in the early 1990s.[94]

The status quo set out in Plan A remained in place. Of the many objections to the idea of detaining asylum seekers that had been set out over the period 1978 to 1979, the most insightful were those expressed by Secretary Engledow. It was clear that the Secretary had thought carefully over this option, because in departmental papers and on the public record he expressed several concerns that have ultimately been borne out in the years since mandatory detention was introduced in 1992. As I have cited earlier in this chapter, Engledow had concluded in 1978 that detention would not deter refugees nor provide 'a final answer' to the flow of boats or to the protection needs of the asylum seekers themselves. He also warned such facilities could create a domestic political problem. And in his speech to the conference on Indochinese refugees at the Australian National University in July 1979, the Secretary had included logical additions to these considerations. 'There is no practicable way we can expect other countries to resettle people from camps in Australia', he said, a point that had already been expressed in Cabinet documents. He then made a further observation that seems prescient in light of the harshness and securitisation of Australia's billion-dollar detention system today. 'There is no practicable way', the Secretary told his audience, 'of forcing people to live in such camps indefinitely, without a tremendous guard apparatus'.[95]

6

Detention

'[B]y their actions and words, our political leaders powerfully shape the sort of country Australia is.'

Paul Keating, 2002

In 1981 the Senate Standing Committee on Foreign Affairs and Defence held an inquiry into Australia's involvement in Indochinese refugee resettlement, building on the original report of 1976. While the Committee concluded that resettlement was 'progressing well', it heard evidence that prejudice against refugees persisted in certain sections of the community, particularly amidst higher than usual levels of unemployment.[1] Derek Volker appeared before the committee on behalf of the Department of Immigration and Ethnic

Affairs, and said that since the beginning of the Indochinese intake, the department had been pleased to observe a 'marked' improvement in community attitudes to this resettlement program. Volker noted, however, that continued public acceptance of the program depended on the government being able to avoid a 'renewed influx' of refugee boats.[2]

The total humanitarian program reached highs of more than 21 000 in 1980–81 and 1981–82, and was then scaled back to just over 17 000 before the Fraser government lost the 1983 election to Hawke's Labor government. By then the refugee intake was coupled with a Special Humanitarian Program (SHP), announced by Macphee in Parliament on 18 November 1981, a category that was intended for persons who needed protection but who fell outside the Convention definition. The UNHCR Branch Office in Sydney had been lobbying 'vigorously' for a broad humanitarian category for several years and it expressed 'immense satisfaction' at the SHP's introduction in 1981.[3] Refugees and SHP entrants now formed the two main components of Australia's humanitarian program, and the program had been placed on the 'permanent footing' that MacKellar had wanted.

In a meeting with Malaysian Foreign Minister Ghazali bin Shafie in Melbourne in late 1981 to discuss the ongoing acceptance of Vietnamese refugees hosted in Malaysia, Minister Macphee expressed his confidence in the humanitarian program. He thought that if the Australian government could carefully manage refugee resettlement to avoid 'resistance' within the community, then in ten years' time, 'Asian migration would not be an issue in Australia'.[4] Yet within just three years, Asian migration would become a source of heated political debate in the Australian Parliament, and by the end of the decade a 'resistance' within the community would irrevocably change the way that governments received asylum seekers arriving by boat.

At the time that Macphee spoke with Ghazali, and continuing into the first years of the Hawke government, the majority of entrants under the humanitarian program were from the Asian region.[5] In addition, after Hawke took office, in 1983–84, one-third of the more than 33 000 people who arrived under the family reunion stream were also from Asia.[6] Meanwhile, the intake of skilled workers in the immigration program (who were primarily from European countries) had been reduced over the late 1970s and early 1980s, in response to changed economic circumstances and a focus on re-skilling existing Australian workers.[7]

The composition of the humanitarian program and family migration stream soon raised objections from some who thought the pace of cultural and demographic change was too fast.[8] Historian Geoffrey Blainey caught the most attention with public comments in March 1984 in which he claimed that Asians were receiving favoured treatment in the immigration program, and that the pace of demographic change was out of step with community opinion.[9] Blainey would come to argue that the government had presented the acceptance of Indochinese refugees to the Australian public as a temporary measure. Many Australians now felt, he wrote in his 1984 book *All for Australia*, that 'a confidence trick had been played upon them', because 'nobody in the years of the boatpeople had mentioned the relatives'.[10] Blainey criticised the Department of Immigration and Ethnic Affairs in particular, for having what he imagined was a 'secret room', in which the real immigration intake was planned, an intake that did not have the approval of the Australian public.[11]

Now in Opposition, the Liberal Party sought to capitalise on the fuss that followed Blainey. Under the leadership of former Foreign Minister Andrew Peacock, the Liberals were dispensing with the Fraser legacy in a range of policy areas. As Paul Kelly detailed in *The End of Certainty*, the move into opposition chimed 'with high unemployment and Asian faces in the suburbs', and the party came to view social tensions caused by economic reform as an 'inevitable cost', and tensions resulting from demographic change as a potential vote-winner.[12] This meant that the bipartisan accord that had underpinned the large post-Second World War immigration program and the move away from a White Australia Policy came unstuck.

Peacock's spokesperson for Immigration was Tasmanian MP Michael Hodgman, known in federal politics as 'the Mouth from the South' and described by Kelly as a 'publicity addict'.[13] Hodgman turned his volume on

Hawke's Minister for Immigration, Stewart West, who was the only left-faction member in Cabinet and thus perceived by Hodgman as a 'weak link' on the Hawke front bench.[14] Spurred on by the government's abolition of a long-standing 'Big Brother' scheme that had brought British boys to Australia, Hodgman led criticism against West for a perceived anti-British bias in the immigration program. Armed with briefing material from his department, West argued that the decrease in settlers from Britain was a drop in individual interest, not a deliberate cutback by government. In Question Time on Tuesday 8 May 1984 Hodgman and several other Opposition MPs implied West was racist, and the debate turned into uproar.

'Rage and tears as the House divides', read headlines the following day.[15] Interjections had flown as West stood at the dispatch box citing the annual statistics on British immigration to Australia. The atmosphere became so tense that Louis Kent, a Labor MP who had seen first-hand the effects of divisive ideology in his native former Yugoslavia, leapt from the back bench in anger and ran down to the floor, hurdling the benches as he went. His cries were duly recorded in Hansard: 'You brought those Asians in and now you're complaining!', Kent yelled. 'You racist bastards!'[16] According to witnesses, Kent had tried to charge at the Opposition members, but was tackled en route by Labor's Mick Young, and 'had to be led from the House to recover'.[17]

Peacock told the House on 10 May that the Opposition was simply questioning the 'mix' of the immigration program, and defended this approach by invoking the Fraser government's record on Indochinese refugee resettlement.[18] West remembered the contrast between the Liberal Party in government and in opposition more bluntly:

> [...] after having done all this, with people like
> Macphee and MacKellar, they then tried to do this
> smart-arse trick, to say that what they had done was
> wrong, [that] there were just too many Asians coming
> here. Because they wanted to try and turn it into an
> election issue in 1984 in my opinion.[19]

Hodgman had indeed released a press statement on 8 May, claiming that 'anyone who dares to disagree' with West risked being branded a racist, and that 'misguided immigration policies' would lose the government 'hundreds of thousands of votes' at the federal election later that year.[20] The *Sydney Morning Herald* predicted Hodgman's attacks could be 'the first taste of the nastiest election campaign' yet.[21] It was not to be. The debate over the composition of the immigration program continued in the parliament and the press for several weeks, until West sought to go on the offensive while also announcing a small increase in skilled migrants.[22] His Shadow shifted tone. After the Hawke government was returned at the polls that December, a sense of bipartisanship resumed and both West and Hodgman were moved to other roles.[23]

Writing in the early 2000s, Andrew Markus, a leading scholar of immigration and social cohesion, marked 1984 as the point at which race entered mainstream modern Australian politics and a conservatism that appealed to prejudice was emboldened.[24] Similarly, in his book *The Eighties*, historian Frank Bongiorno set out how the 'Blainey debate' combined with a struggle on Indigenous land rights to make 1984 a 'critical moment' in modern Australian history, the end of a bipartisanship on race.[25] And in this process, a fissure between the moderate and conservative wings of the Liberal Party had become apparent.[26] For his part, Macphee had backed West's vision for the portfolio.[27] The two were not close in the same way that Macphee and Young were, but after the emotions of that particular Question Time the mild-mannered former Minister had gone to see West, and passionately disowned his own side's line of attack:

> Macphee just walked straight into my office and [said] […] 'Stewie you know I'm not with them on this, I mean I deplore what they're doing, I support you, just keep going, you're going alright on it – and ignore those bastards'.[28]

The acceptance of settlers from Asia did keep going, but according to Jupp, Blainey's arguments – around the influence of special interest groups, a perceived overly generous refugee intake and the pace of community opinion – had 'set the tone' for future criticism of immigration policy and multiculturalism.[29] And internal divisions within the Liberal Party over these issues came on public display in 1988, when Hawke strategically put a motion to Parliament on 25 August that acknowledged the historic bipartisanship underpinning the long shift away from White Australia –'to the overwhelming national, and international, benefit of Australia' – and reaffirmed the government's commitment to non-discriminatory policy.[30] John Howard, the Opposition leader at the time, had been suggesting that the intake of settlers from Asia was exceeding the expectations of some sections of the Australian community, and told the media that he could not support the motion's final line, which read as follows:

> That this House [...] gives its unambiguous
> and unqualified commitment to the principle
> that, whatever criteria are applied by Australian
> Governments in exercising their sovereign right to
> determine the composition of the immigration intake,
> race or ethnic origin shall never, explicitly or implicitly,
> be among them.[31]

Howard opposed these words, arguing that they implied government did not have a sovereign right to decide who entered the country.[32] When the division was called Mac-Kellar walked out of the chamber, and three other Opposition MPs crossed the floor to vote with the government, including Macphee and the future Minister for Immigration Phillip Ruddock.[33] Howard was replaced as Opposition leader the following year by Peacock, who affirmed party support for a non-discriminatory immigration policy, but Macphee lost party pre-selection for his long-held safe Liberal seat of Goldstein.[34]

The politics of race and immigration would find renewed voice following Howard's election as Prime Minister in 1996, and his tolerance for the uproar caused by a new commentator on Asian immigration, in the form of Independent MP Pauline Hanson.[35] Hanson would echo Blainey's claims of 'reverse discrimination' in government policy. But in the meantime, as Bongiorno wrote, the immigration debates of the 1980s had laid bare an insecurity about who Australians were and wanted to be.[36] Entry policy was part of a broader debate over the concept of multiculturalism and its role in national identity.[37] Abandoning White Australia was one thing, but the reality of demographic change was another.[38] As noted later in this chapter, asylum seekers in the Hawke and Keating years became a focal point for community resentment against migration from Asia.

The question of sovereign control over entry, a central

element of Hawke's motion to Parliament, soon turned toward Australia's obligations to refugees. From the late 1980s onward, there ensued what experts in migration law and policy have called a 'high profile interbranch dispute' between the courts and the Parliament.[39] Under the *Administrative Decisions (Judicial Review) Act 1977* (Cth), the Minister for Immigration's discretion on the outcome of protection claims was increasingly opened to judicial oversight.[40] Notably, in September 1989, the High Court of Australia handed down its judgment in the case of *Chan Yee Kin*, in which it determined that the term 'persecution' under Article 1(A)(2) of the Refugee Convention had a wider interpretation than government had previously applied.

The Department of Immigration saw the judgment in Chan as having 'significant implications', believing it challenged the traditional notion that government, not the courts, had ultimate control over the admission of refugees.[41] Then a senior member of the department under Immigration Minister Senator Robert Ray, Wayne Gibbons saw the implications of the *Administrative Decisions (Judicial Review) Act* (commonly referred to as ADJR) as reaching to the heart of debates over the role of immigration in changing Australian society. In our interview in 2011, he explained his view that government could 'hasten the timetable for the evolution of a multicultural society' only if it 'controlled all the levers' of entry.[42] Gibbons argued that the Act posed 'a major challenge to a government that's trying to

keep the public onside with a broadening immigration program'. Mary Crock, who has written extensively on changes
in Australian migration law during this period, believes that
the Australian government came to view its Convention
obligations as 'a direct threat' to its control of the migration
program.[43]

Until the end of the 1980s Australia had received very
few applications for refugee status – just a few hundred each
year. This changed very quickly when, in 1989, the government of the People's Republic of China (PRC) suppressed
pro-democracy protesters at Tiananmen Square in early June
and Hawke made a sudden announcement that Chinese
temporarily in Australia would have their stay extended.
Hawke's announcement encompassed some 20 000 students
from the PRC and several thousand others in Australia,
many of whom submitted claims for protection to DORS.[44]
James Jupp and Glenn Nicholls have both observed that at
a time when other Western states were facing an increase in
asylum claims due to conflict and geo-political change in
parts of Europe and other areas of the world, the Australian
government created its own workload through an on-the-
spot political decision.[45]

It was against this backdrop that, from November 1989
onwards, asylum seekers from South-East Asia began to
reach Australia by boat once more. The first of these boats
sailed from Cambodia, a country ravaged by conflict, the
genocidal reign of the Khmer Rouge and, since the end of

the 1970s, occupation by the Socialist Republic of Vietnam.[46] Cambodia was not part of the Comprehensive Plan of Action. It was, however, the subject of an internationally negotiated peace process, an effort to secure accord between the Vietnamese-backed State of Cambodia (formerly People's Republic of Kampuchea) and resistance forces (including the Khmer Rouge). When Vietnamese forces fulfilled a pledge to withdraw from Cambodia in September 1989, international media reported unrest and uncertainty in the country, a fear that conflict would intensify and spark a flight of people into the region.[47]

In the early afternoon of 28 October 1989, two extended families and three crew members boarded a 13-metre fishing boat at the port of Kompong Som, on the southern coast of Cambodia, and set out into the Gulf of Thailand.[48] Among those onboard were a five-year-old boy and his eighty-year-old grandmother. One of the passengers kept a diary of the journey, which was translated by Australian authorities. In their notes, the diarist is identified as twenty-two-year-old Lim Chu Kheng, a name that would become well known in a High Court decision three years later. The diary and other investigations into their journey indicated that the families steered to Singapore and then down to Jakarta, purchasing fuel with United States dollars at islands along the way. On reaching the Indonesian capital their boat was boarded by police; authorities gave them boxes of noodles, salted fish, water and 900 litres of fuel, and charts and maps (including one from a school atlas) with directions to Australia.[49] An Indonesian patrol vessel (reportedly a gift from Australia) escorted them out of the harbour on 15 November.[50] Hugging the coast eastward, the families and crew were given papaya and mango as locals sailed to their boat. They continued on and saw the lights of Bali – it was an 'amazing view', the young diarist thought. The group then turned and took to the open sea; through three nights of frightening weather and waves that almost capsized their tiny craft, they made it to the coastline of Western Australia on 25 November.[51]

Pender Bay is more than six hours north of Broome, and it was here that the boat became lodged near the shallows and could not be moved. Eventually, sighting a car in the distance, three of the crew swam 500 metres to shore; they told the driver they were from Kampuchea.[52] Customs officials arrived and the 'Pender Bay', as the group and its boat became known, were escorted to Broome.[53]

Authorities quickly took the view that 'publicity about this boat may encourage others'.[54] A Customs officer told the *West Australian* newspaper that if the passengers were indeed Cambodian refugees, he feared more would be tempted to make the journey.[55] This news report was printed around a large close-up of the grandmother looking out of the boat next to two smiling children, their young faces beaming with happiness at the photographer. By late December 1989 the asylum seekers from the Pender Bay were placed in unfenced accommodation at Villawood Immigration Detention Centre, from which they were not permitted to leave.[56] Administrative detention at this point was discretionary rather than mandatory, as detailed by legal scholar Eve Lester in her book *Making Migration Law: The foreigner, sovereignty and the case of Australia*. In 1990 two more boats carrying Cambodians made it to Australia, the first landing off Broome in April and the second spotted sinking in international waters 260 kilometres north-west of Darwin in June, its seventeen children and sixty-two adults rescued by the naval patrol vessel HMAS *Townsville*.[57] Their arrival brought the number of Cambodians seeking protection to 224.[58]

The following year, in 1991, the Department of Immigration, Local Government and Ethnic Affairs' annual report included a ten-page feature setting out in detail what happened when a boat was on the horizon. The piece was similar in tone to the text and photographs within the department's annual reports of the late 1970s, but it was also an attempt to counter media controversy over the department's treatment of the Cambodian asylum seekers during the previous year (a subject examined later in this chapter). The feature thus recounted how, through urgent phone calls and early-morning flights, the department would muster together a team of Immigration officers, media liaison staff and interpreters from around Australia at short notice, while other staff would travel hours aboard a Customs vessel to meet and escort the asylum seekers to land. The department's

Director of Media Liaison, Gordon Benjamin, added an informal account of his experience seeing two boats land at Darwin in March 1991. Benjamin sought to convey a sense of camaraderie and hard work on the part of those officials who brought the asylum seekers to shore:

> Those of us privileged to have witnessed a boat
> arrival can report a mixture of emotions: adrenalin-
> stirring excitement at the thought of the processing
> challenges ahead; apprehension at the thought of
> extraordinarily long hours on the job with tough-on-
> the-spot decision-making; admiration for the people
> who have undertaken and survived such a long and
> no-doubt dangerous journey; sympathy for the babies
> and toddlers undergoing bewildering experiences
> in unfamiliar surroundings; and annoyance that yet
> another group of people has chosen to 'crash the
> frontier' in this unorthodox and unauthorized way.[59]

The text was accompanied by a photo of children and elderly asylum seekers who arrived a few weeks later, in April 1991, from Cambodia, Vietnam and the PRC. The photo had been snapped at a short distance by the *Northern Territory News* while the asylum seekers were sitting on plastic chairs awaiting initial processing. Another image showed the department's Northern Territory Regional Manager, Malcolm Paterson, crouching down to carefully lift a nine-month-old baby out of the arms of a Customs inspector on a vessel below. The following year, in 1992, the department's annual report included a photograph of a former South Vietnamese army officer, who had arrived on that same 17-metre fishing boat in April 1991. The photo was courtesy of the *West Australian* newspaper. The caption in the department's annual report stated that Thuc Van Nguyen had been jailed for twelve years in Vietnam; the Department of Immigration had initially rejected his claim for protection and placed him in detention. Now, relaxed and smiling at the camera, he had been released. Under policy introduced under Minister for Immigration Gerry Hand, Nguyen had not received permanent protection, but instead was granted a four-year temporary entry permit.[60]

Despite the sympathy Benjamin expressed for those who risked the journey, the idea that asylum seekers were 'crashing the frontier' was ever present. The ten-page feature of 1991 harked back to the same concerns that had been raised with Immigration by the US State Department in 1978:

> [The department's] first priority when a boat arrives
> is to ensure the basic needs of the boatpeople are
> attended to: that they receive medical care, food,
> clothing and shelter. The response is balanced
> carefully against the knowledge that Australian
> reception arrangements are seen in Asia as signals

of the Australian Government's attitude towards boat arrivals.[61]

Reception arrangements were perceived as sending a 'signal' to both prospective asylum seekers and to an Australian public unnerved by their arrival. The concern was long-standing, as the archival records from the Fraser era show, and now it was exacerbated by an increased awareness of smuggling operations out of ports on the southern coast of China, among other locations in the region.[62] Immigration reported that it had uncovered false claims among some of the new arrivals, and claimed a small number of people on later vessels had misrepresented their nationalities.[63] The concern was also exacerbated by the issues that had so inflamed parliament and the press during the 1980s. Wayne Gibbons was now a Deputy Secretary under Minister Hand, and held the belief that control of entry meant having some control over the public's response to demographic change:

> I maintained this very strongly during my time as a policy advisor, you've got to keep control of those areas that allow you the political freedom to be adventurous with immigration. If you don't control some things to keep the core racists at bay [...] you won't get very far with immigration.[64]

Gibbons told a parliamentary committee that a relaxation of entry controls would send 'a great signal to the world which might result in large numbers turning up and trying their luck'.[65] This view was shared by Ian Simington, who held senior roles under Minister Senator Ray and Minister Hand. In a piece published by the Australian National University in 1989, Simington had expressed a view that migration from under-developed to developed countries was an increasing phenomenon; for millions of people 'the proposition is simple', he had argued: 'rather than stay at home and starve or suffer [...] you move to another country in the hope of a better life'.[66] In this same piece Simington had mused on the potential for population movement with the end of British rule in Hong Kong in 1997.[67] The view may have been shared by Minister Hand, who disapproved of Hawke granting extension of stay to the PRC students. Hand suggested to Cabinet colleagues in 1992 that the unplanned extension 'could ultimately produce up to a million Chinese immigrants'.[68]

Writing in 1993, immigration scholar Bob Birrell noted that it was the few hundred Cambodian asylum seekers, more than the thousands of PRC students, who were perceived as the greatest challenge to the government's control of entry because of the manner of their arrival.[69] Labor Senator Jim McKiernan, who was a member of the Joint Standing Committee on Migration, went so far as to describe asylum seekers' lack of authorised arrival as 'a direct attack on Australia's national sovereignty'.[70] But the Cambodians' cases were viewed within government as particularly unwelcome because the Australian government was closely involved in the international efforts to secure a peace settlement in Cambodia. Their cases became overtly politicised on 6 June 1990, when Prime Minister Hawke made comments in a television interview that the Cambodians were not political refugees and would be returned home.[71] Hawke insisted that people who 'pull up stumps, get in a boat and lob in Australia' were engaged in 'economic refugeeism'.[72] Although Minister Hand later sought to distance himself from Hawke's comments, claiming he corrected the Prime Minister in 'colourful' terms, Foreign Minister Gareth Evans made similar statements to journalists in Canberra on 15 June.[73] A peace settlement in Cambodia was central to the Foreign Minister's ambitions to establish Australia as 'an activist middle power' in Asia.[74] Three days after Evans made these comments, DORS rejected the applications of the Cambodians from the Pender Bay. By this point, the asylum seekers had been held in detention for more than six months.[75]

At this very same time, the Department of Immigration, Local Government and Ethnic Affairs was actively exploring whether the Cambodians could be sent back, or whether Cambodia's Hun Sen government could discourage people from leaving.[76] In early 1992 Minister Hand travelled to Cambodia to inspect the situation for himself, and would later argue that because the peace process involved the return of hundreds of thousands of Cambodians from Thai camps, Australia could not simultaneously say that 'everybody that comes here by boat can automatically stay'.[77] Legal scholar Penelope Mathew has noted that Australia's obligations under the Refugee Convention meant that it could not simply declare Cambodia a safe country for the purpose of returning asylum seekers, but had to engage in fair, principled and individual determinations of their refugee status.[78] Their right to such determinations was thus taken up by a small but growing community of migration lawyers.

The possibility that protection claims could extend outside a departmental conference room and into the courts had been raised many years earlier, at one of the planning sessions for DORS back in October 1977. That day the assembled departmental representatives had talked over how the new procedures would accommodate the need for applicants to access legal advice, and the potential for delays and lengthy appeals by unsuccessful claimants or persons with manifestly unfounded applications. Over the course of the discussion there arose the following observation:

> Difficulties were foreseen in the proposed procedures
> breeding a new race of 'immigration lawyers',
> marked by their skill in delaying official procedures
> by exploiting appeal mechanisms and in other ways
> obstructing fair determination by the committee.

> It was decided that we would have to live with this
> prospect, in the interests of providing and being seen
> to provide the applicant with every opportunity to
> present a full and favourable case.[79]

Simington was at this meeting as a representative from Prime
Minister and Cabinet, before his move to Immigration.
More than fifteen years later, he worked as a senior adviser
to Minister Hand, and in 1993 both men were called to give
evidence in a high-profile case before the Federal Court that
heard allegations of 'institutional bias' against three Cambodian asylum seekers.[80] In an interview with Bob Birrell
conducted that year, Hand expressed a resentment of the
lawyers who appealed his department's decisions. They were
a 'classic type', he said, a type who wears skinny jeans, sees
themselves as a 'radical' in a contest with his department,
and 'bitches and belly aches on the national airwaves' about
the plight of their clients.[81]

Hailing from the Labor Party's left faction, Hand was
described by Keating's Minister for Social Security Neal
Blewett as 'passionate, stubborn, argumentative' and 'impossible to dislike'.[82] In *A Cabinet Diary*, Blewett's record of the
first Keating government, he wrote that Hand was engaged
in a series of 'hasty ad hoc expedients cobbled together to
stem the flood'.[83] These expedients have been extensively
detailed by Crock, Mathew, and Savitri Taylor among others,
and (as previously mentioned) included the introduction of

temporary entry permits instead of permanent protection for those found to be refugees.[84] It also included the establishment of a detention centre at Port Hedland, more than 600 kilometres from Broome on Australia's remote northwest coastline, and the transfer of some asylum seekers from one detention centre to another, further and further away from community networks, media and legal representatives.

In 1993 one of the Cambodians who arrived on the Pender Bay made an individual communication to the UN Human Rights Committee, which set out how these transfers had occurred. The author, identified as 'A', had been placed in Villawood on 21 December 1989. After DORS rejected his claim in June 1990, and a subsequent appeals process, he was transferred to a flood-prone site 85 kilometres outside Darwin in mid-1991, during which his ability to talk to other detainees was reportedly curtailed and his permission to make phone calls refused. On 6 August 1991 he was moved to another camp much closer to Darwin; and, finally, he was removed to the newly designated, basic facility at Port Hedland in Western Australia in October 1991.[85]

Created out of former miners' accommodation blocks, the Port Hedland Immigration Reception and Processing Centre was intentionally close to the arrival points of the asylum seekers.[86] This idea was not new. For example, in 1985, five Irian Jayan men reached Australia and lodged protection claims (risking diplomatic controversy with Indonesia), and amid concern for further arrivals from that province, the Department of Foreign Affairs had advised Foreign Minister Bill Hayden that Australia could consider asking Papua New Guinea to establish a camp, 'where those heading for Australia could be held while their bona fides as refugees were examined'.[87]

Remote detention at Port Hedland was an attempt to signal to prospective asylum seekers that they should not assume landing in Australia would mean remaining in Australia. This was the same basic message authorities had sought to convey to Vietnamese boat arrivals several years earlier, but it was now in a very different form. The remote location also served the purpose of isolating asylum seekers from support networks in the capital cities. In 1993 the Department of Immigration, Local Government and Ethnic Affairs gave evidence to the Joint Standing Committee on Migration's inquiry into asylum, border control and detention that if asylum seekers were held in detention in large population centres, this 'could prematurely signal [their] acceptance into the community'.[88] Legal and other service providers submitted to the parliamentary inquiry that the isolated location hindered detainees' access to interpreters, counsellors, and medical, religious and social services versed in cross-cultural communication.[89] 'A' submitted to the Human Rights Committee that the increasing remoteness of his detention 'vastly compounded' his difficulties in accessing legal advice (a claim that Australia countered in its own submission).[90]

In 1992 a case was pursued in the Federal Court on behalf of several of the asylum seekers, challenging the grounds for their detention.[91] Hand moved quickly to ensure the detention of boat arrivals was enshrined in law. In Cabinet in late April, just days before the case was to be heard, Blewett recorded that the usually likeable Hand was 'all over the place', full of 'vivid anecdotes on the wickedness of the boat people and their sinister manipulators', and critical of the churches and 'do-gooders' that sought to help them.[92] Blewett had the impression that Hand's portfolio was 'a disaster area'.[93] Keating told journalist Kerry O'Brien years later that from what he had understood at the time, the Department of Immigration was 'losing track of people' before it could check their health and 'bona fides as refugees'.[94]

At this Cabinet meeting Hand proposed to create a legislative basis for detaining asylum seekers who arrived by boat without a valid visa. According to Keating, the proposal went through 'virtually without debate', a curious and disappointing performance from a Prime Minister who claimed to value the Cabinet process as a way to intellectually frame and critique arguments. Keating told O'Brien that he believed Hand's left-faction credentials meant the human rights implications of the legislation had been taken into account.[95] Whatever the process that day, the Cabinet's decision led to the passage of the *Migration Amendment Act 1992* (Cth) under which detention of these asylum

seekers became mandatory and non-reviewable; the legislation appeared to limit detention to a maximum of 273
days, but as Lester has detailed, custody could be prolonged
beyond this point during certain stages of the application
process.[96]

In the Minister's second reading speech, on 5 May 1992,
Hand told Parliament that the most important aspect of the
legislation was that the courts could not 'interfere with custody'.[97] Notably, Hand's desire to avoid legal intervention
had the support of former Minister MacKellar, who asserted
his view that lawyers and the courts had 'taken control of
the program away from the minister and the government of
the day'.[98]

Hand also told Parliament the legislation was 'only
intended to be an interim measure', designed to address 'the
pressing requirements of the current situation' by placing
the boat arrivals into a facility (Keating later said he had
understood it to be 'a temporary holding point').[99] But
Hand took a definitive step later that year, and secured the
passage of the *Migration Reform Act 1992* (Cth) to mandate detention for all unlawful non-citizens (those without a
valid visa). The Act was not proclaimed in its entirety until
1994, at which point it removed the time limits under the
previous legislation.

In late 1992 the constitutionality of the detention
regime first put in place for the Cambodians was largely
upheld by the High Court in the case of *Chu Kheng Lim*.

While the High Court found that the Parliament could not entirely exclude review by the courts, the legislation was otherwise 'a valid use of government power' as its purpose was to facilitate removal or processing of the individual, and was not punitive.[100] The deterrent value that had been debated more than a decade earlier in Washington and in Canberra was thus obscured.

No matter the remoteness of the facility or the legislative basis for detention, it soon became clear that the measure did not deter people who needed protection. Slightly fewer than 400 asylum seekers would sail to Australia in 1992–93 and 1993–94, fleeing from Vietnam, the PRC and farther afield.[101] And in the meantime, some of those who had arrived on the Pender Bay were held in detention for more than four years.[102] A number of babies were born in detention, and a number of detained asylum seekers staged hunger strikes or other physical protests.[103]

When the aforementioned Joint Standing Committee inquiry into detention reported in 1994, it largely supported existing practice but acknowledged that 'difficulties have arisen' because facilities designed for the short-term provision of basic needs had transformed into long-term accommodation.[104] Then in 1997, the UN Human Rights Committee concluded in the case of *A v Australia* that A's detention had constituted a violation of the prohibition on arbitrary detention, under Article 9(1) of the International Covenant on Civil and Political Rights. The Committee also found that A's right to have his detention reviewed by a court, under Article 9(4) of the Covenant had been violated.[105]

Reflecting on the move to mandatory detention, scholars have noted both its failure to address the needs of vulnerable people, and its basis as a domestic response to a complex regional (and global) phenomenon. Andreas Schloenhardt, an expert in migration in the Asia-Pacific, has described mandatory detention as part of a simplistic criminalisation of irregular migration by the Australian government, one that has since failed to address the reasons why people flee, or the needs (and number) of asylum seekers in the region.[106] In 2016, Andrew Carr, of the Strategic and Defence Studies Centre at the Australian National University, wrote that despite the Keating government's emphasis on engagement with Asia, it chose to respond to asylum seekers with domestic legislative and policy mechanisms rather than pursuing a co-operative regional response, in the manner of the Fraser government (with the boat-holding arrangements) or (somewhat differently to Fraser) the Howard and Gillard governments (through the 'Bali Process').[107]

As Australia's detention network expanded through the 2000s, and is maintained today, studies have found that mandatory detention may have compounded adverse public opinion on asylum seekers. By removing vulnerable individuals from public view, they appear in the media as a homogenous and distant group, and this diminishes public empathy for their plight.[108] Scholars Nick Haslam and Anne Pedersen have found that this form of dehumanisation plays a central role in public opinion on asylum seekers.[109] Furthermore, studies have shown that detention can foster an impression that the detained person has done something wrong, or poses a threat to the community, an image further strengthened by references to asylum seekers as 'illegal entrants' in contemporary political debate.[110]

In 2015, in the interview with O'Brien, Keating explained away his Cabinet's decisions to endorse mandatory detention by saying that the issue had 'no heat' in it at the time. Certainly the number of asylum seekers arriving by boat during Hand's tenure as Minister was quite small, just one or two hundred a year aboard a handful of vessels, and was surpassed not only by the number of asylum seeker claimants who had arrived by air, but most importantly, paled in comparison to the tens of thousands of applications for protection received by other states parties.[111] Evidence of this 'heat' was reported (or fuelled), however, by some MPs whose constituents were said to be aggrieved at their inability to sponsor family into the country, or who were struggling in a time of high unemployment, and expressed their resentment against the 'Asian boat people'.[112]

Grievances over fairness or competition for jobs had been aired before, as chapter 1 of this book showed, and as such they highlight the role of political leaders in assuaging (or endorsing) community disquiet about asylum seekers arriving by boat. Keating himself has drawn direct attention to this role: in a speech in 2002 he criticised the Howard government for having marginalised asylum seekers to the point that 'it is acceptable in Australia for children to be locked away, out of sight, in desert camps and treated like prisoners'.[113] Keating told his audience that he believed 'by their actions and words, our political leaders powerfully shape the sort of country Australia is'. One could add to this that a political leader's lack of action or words on a subject as sensitive as the detention of children, women and men, can shape the sort of country Australia becomes.

How did we get here?

At first glance, some of the evidence presented in this book may challenge the popular view that Australia responded well to the Vietnamese who arrived by boat in the late 1970s and early 1980s. Lists setting out options for turning back boats or detaining asylum seekers seem uncomfortably similar to contemporary policy, and far removed from a positive image of the Fraser era. But in fact, this evidence makes that image much more compelling, because those policy options were not adopted despite the domestic political challenge that the boats represented. Further, the first-hand detail within UNHCR records enriches our understanding of the way that Australia observed its Convention obligations in relation to the Vietnamese boat arrivals, both in determining their status and the way it received them once they reached Australian shores.

Most importantly, because options for turning back boats or establishing detention centres were put to paper, so too were the arguments against them, throwing into sharp relief the harsh and ill-conceived nature of the deterrent policies that are today endorsed by both major parties in Australia. Questions that were unresolved forty years ago (if a boat was turned around, where would the people onboard sail to?), remain a source of great uncertainty and concern today, while assessments back then (detention would not provide a final answer) have now been borne out – to the mental and physical detriment of some of the several thousand men, women and children who have been held in Australia's network of detention facilities under a 'tremendous guard apparatus', and to the detriment of public understanding as to why these people risked a long journey in search of protection.

It is easy to say that we cannot compare then and now, that the nature of asylum seeking and forced migration has changed too much in the last forty years. Certainly things have changed, including a decreased willingness on the part of many states to admit asylum seekers. But the obligation to treat vulnerable people with dignity and humanity remains. And so too does the fact that Australia receives just a fraction of the asylum seekers who are hosted by, or claiming protection in, other countries around the world.

In November 2016 the United Nations Special Rapporteur on the human rights of migrants, François Crépeau, conducted an official visit to Australia. His subsequent report to the UN Human Rights Council noted that Australia's current asylum policies 'blemish' the country's otherwise 'good human rights record'.[1] This record is partly informed by Australia's response to the Indochinese refugee situation. In 1980 the Department of Foreign Affairs stated in its annual report that 'successive Australian governments have established a very high standing for Australia on refugee matters', and 'refugee policy is now an important part of our foreign relations'.[2] The following year, in a submission to the 1981 Senate inquiry on Indochinese resettlement, the same department put this good record in context, admitting that Australia's acceptance of refugees probably had greater significance at home than abroad, and that 'the reaction of many countries to Australia's record would probably be, "we would expect nothing less"'.[3]

For a country that managed to respond humanely to just over 2000 people arriving by boat, the move to mandatory detention is all the more striking for having been precipitated by just a few hundred asylum seekers who sought protection in the same way. It seems that while the arrival of Vietnamese refugees by boat prompted the expansion of Australia's refugee resettlement program, and through it the non-discriminatory immigration program, by the early 1990s, following heated political debate over Asian immigration, a hard line against the next group of asylum seekers was viewed by decision makers in government as the only way to preserve what had been achieved in that previous era. This thinking set aside, of course, the evidence that in responding to the Vietnamese boat arrivals, Australia was able to observe international law while still pursuing a self-interested desire to both offset international criticism and manage the movement of asylum seekers.

The question that Fraser posed to me, 'what else could you do?', is as relevant as ever. The other answers to that question have been implemented, but not in a way that addresses the needs of vulnerable people and Australia's international responsibilities. The Special Rapporteur found Australia's current asylum policy to be 'regressive' and falling behind international standards. His report is one of several such investigations in recent years – by international agencies, human rights organisations and parliamentary committees – to note the inherent risk of *refoulement* in the practice of turning back boats, and to set out the mental anguish, trauma and prolonged uncertainty experienced by many children, women and men in Australia's onshore and offshore detention system. Most notably, the Special Rapporteur concluded that in terms of human rights, Australia's system of offshore detention and processing was 'not salvageable'.[4] Clearly, current policy has not provided a viable answer to the challenge of displacement. Because forced migration is not something that can be 'solved' as such, but something to be managed, through rational public debate, compassionate reception procedures, and fair and efficient status determination, then surely that points back to a principled response.

Acknowledgments

The publication of this book was made possible thanks to an Australian Academy of the Humanities Publication Subsidy, and the research process was supported and assisted by the Kaldor Centre for International Law at UNSW. My sincere appreciation goes to the team at NewSouth, especially Phillipa McGuinness, Deborah Nixon and Jocelyn Hungerford, as well as to the staff at the National Archives of Australia, who aided my research through grants, patience and unique expertise. The original idea for this book arose through my doctoral research at the University of Oxford, an experience that would not have been possible without the support of Merton College Oxford and the Clarendon Fund.

This book is the result of a long learning process, shaped not only by time spent in the archives but also through countless conversations with friends, colleagues and interviewees, whose perspectives ensured that my understanding of the subject continued to evolve. To my mentor and doctoral supervisor Professor Deborah Oxley, who challenged my thinking and fostered my love for history, and to Dr David Meredith, and Chloe and Ted Oxley – thank you.

I would like to thank my talented colleagues at the Kaldor Centre, and am very grateful to Professor Jane McAdam for her expert guidance in the drafting stages. Many thanks, too, to Professor James Jupp, who provided valuable advice on draft chapters and wisdom along the way, and to Professor Guy S Goodwin-Gill for pointing me toward his remarkable UNHCR files and supporting my research. And I am especially grateful to have had the unfailing encouragement, generosity and example of the Hon. Ian Macphee.

For gracious proofreading and feedback, I would like to thank Derek Volker, Dr Eve Lester, Garry Woodard, Dr Joyce Chia, Nyrie Palmer, Lauren Martin, Khanh Hoang, Loretta Grace, Dr Andrew Cichy, Alice Pailthorpe and Dr Máté Rigó, among many others whose thoughtfulness made all the difference during the last months of the writing process. My love and gratitude goes to Mary-Beth and Terry Higgins, and Maureen and Terry Davies for all their support.

Notes

Introduction

1   'Aid for refugee ships', the *Straits Times*, 5 May 1975, 1.
2   'Aid for refugee ships'; Australia. EG Whitlam, *Commonwealth Parliamentary Debates*, House of Representatives, 15 May 1975, 2307.
3   P Lee, 'Medical aid, food for refugees', the *Straits Times*, 6 May 1975, 1; '25 refugee ships anchor off Singapore', the *New York Times*, 5 May 1975, 12; '36 refugee vessels at Singapore await, food, fuel, water', the *New York Times*, 6 May 1975, 18.
4   'Thousands of refugees fleeing on Vietnamese boats appeal for food and water', the *New York Times*, 3 May 1975, 12.
5   G Yeend, 'Royal Interocean Lines', 8 May 1975, National Archives of Australia (hereafter NAA), M4797 1.
6   G Yeend, 'Vietnamese refugees in Singapore', 9 May 1975, NAA, M4797 1. See also: Australia. Senate Standing Committee on Foreign Affairs and Defence, *Australia and the Refugee Problem*, Australian Government Publishing Service, Canberra, 1976, 7.
7   G Yeend, 'Vietnamese refugees in Singapore'.
8   G Yeend, 'Vietnamese refugees in Singapore'.
9   P Weller, *Malcolm Fraser PM: A study in prime ministerial power in Australia*, Penguin, Melbourne, 1989, 39.
10   G Yeend, 'Vietnamese refugees in Singapore'.
11   J Jupp, *From White Australia to Woomera*, Cambridge University Press, New York, 2002, 17; F Hawkins, *Critical Years in Immigration: Canada and Australia compared*, New South Wales University Press, Sydney, 1988, xxxvii. See also: K Cronin, 'A culture of control: An overview of

immigration policy-making', in J Jupp and M Kabala (eds), *The Politics of Australian Immigration,* Australian Government Publishing Service, Canberra, 1993, 84.

12 United Nations, Vienna Convention on the Law of Treaties, 23 May 1969, 1155 UNTS 331 (Art. 31(1)); UN General Assembly, Convention Relating to the Status of Refugees, 28 July 1951, 189 UNTS 137.

13 P Mares, *Borderline: Australia's treatment of refugees and asylum seekers,* UNSW Press, Sydney, 2001, 4.

14 Mares, *Borderline,* 27. See also: N Viviani, *The Indochinese in Australia, 1975 to 1995: From burnt boats to barbecues,* Oxford University Press, Melbourne, 1996, 5.

15 Australia. Senate Standing Committee on Foreign Affairs and Defence, *Australia and the Refugee Problem,* 7.

16 'Contingency planning for unauthorised arrival of Vietnamese refugees', 19 May 1975, NAA A1209 1975/1689.

17 'Contingency planning for unauthorised arrival of Vietnamese refugees'.

18 K Neumann, 'Oblivious to the obvious? Australian asylum-seeker policies and the use of the past', in K Neumann and G Tavan (eds), *Does History Matter? Making and debating citizenship, immigration and refugee policy in Australia and New Zealand,* ANU Press, Canberra, 2009, 47–48.

19 MJ Gibney, *The Ethics and Politics of Asylum: Liberal democracy and the response to refugees,* Cambridge University Press, Cambridge, 2004, 167.

20 United Nations High Commissioner for Human Rights, *Opening Statement by Zeid Ra'ad Al Hussein United Nations High Commissioner for Human Rights at the Human Rights Council 27th Session,* 8 September 2014, <www.ohchr.org/EN/NewsEvents/Pages/DisplayNews.aspx?NewsID=14998>, accessed 30 April 2017.

21 For example, see further: O Laughland, 'Malcolm Fraser on Coalition asylum plans: No limits to the inhumanity', the *Guardian,* Australian edition, 16 August 2013, <www.theguardian.com/world/2013/aug/16/malcolm-fraser-coalition-asylum-policy>, accessed 12 July 2017; M Fraser, 'Vietnamese refugees were a boon not a burden', the *Age,* 29 July 2013, <www.theage.com.au/federal-politics/political-opinion/vietnamese-refugees-were-a-boon-not-a-burden-20130728-2qsh4.html>, accessed 12 July 2017.

22 Interview with M Fraser, 14 December 2010, Melbourne (transcript with author).

23 Weller, *Malcolm Fraser PM,* 51.

24 Interview with M Fraser.

25 M Fraser, Draft statement, undated circa September 1977, NAA M4797 9 Correspondence.

26 R Manne, 'Tragedy of errors: Australia's shipwrecked refugee policy', the *Monthly* (March 2013); R Manne, 'Asylum seekers', the *Monthly* (September 2010); M Steketee, 'Malcolm Fraser the unsung hero of

humane refugee policy', the *Australian*, 2 January 2010.

27   M Steketee, 'History not always meant to be easy', the *Australian*, 20 March 2010, <www.theaustralian.com.au/arts/books/history-not-always-meant-to-be-easy/story-e6frg8nf-1225841454998>, accessed 12 July 2017.

28   For example, see further: HGP Colebatch, 'The left re-writes its history on refugees', *Quadrant*, 54(10), 2010; R Stevens, *Immigration Policy from 1970 to the Present*, Routledge Studies in Modern History, Oxford, 2016, 108–120; K Stats, 'Welcome to Australia? A reappraisal of the Fraser government's approach to refugees, 1975–83', *Australian Journal of International Affairs*, 69(1), 2014, 69–87; J Smit, 'Malcolm Fraser's response to commercial refugee voyages', *Journal of International Relations*, 8(2), 2010, 76–103; S Macintyre, 'Fear of invasion has given way to fear of the refugee', the *Age*, 20 June 2003, <www.theage.com.au/articles/2003/06/19/1055828433377.html>, accessed 17 April 2017. See also: B York, 'The myth of our humanitarian tradition', the *Age*, 27 June 2003, <www.theage.com.au/articles/2003/06/26/1056449364608.html>, accessed 12 July 2017.

29   G Sheridan, 'Malcolm Fraser was no saint for Vietnamese refugees', the *Australian*, 26 March 2015, <www.theaustralian.com.au/opinion/columnists/greg-sheridan/malcolm-fraser-was-no-saint-for-vietnamese-refugees/news-story/0bb05ec963130f091dd983c917e8cf76>, accessed 12 July 2017.

30   N Viviani, *The Long Journey: Vietnamese migration and settlement in Australia*, Melbourne University Press, Melbourne, 1984, 113. See also: Viviani, *The Indochinese in Australia*, 8–9.

31   M Crock, 'Refugees in Australia: Of lore, legends and the judicial process', presented at the Annual Colloquium of the Australian Judicial Conference, Darwin, NT, 31 May 2003, 8; Jupp, *From White Australia to Woomera*, 43, 45; Gibney, *The Ethics and Politics of Asylum*, 167; Mares, *Borderline*, 73.

32   E Feller, 'The war on boats: Let's bring facts to national conversation', *Pursuit*, University of Melbourne, 7 November 2016.

33   M MacKellar, 'The international implications of immigration and refugee policy', *Heindorff Memorial Lecture*, Queensland Branch, Institute for International Affairs, Brisbane, 4 June 1979; Australia. Department of Immigration and Ethnic Affairs, *Review '78*, Australian Government Publishing Service, Canberra, 1978, 26.

34   N Viviani, 'The Vietnamese in Australia: New problems in old forms', in IH Burnley, S Encel and G McCall (eds), *Immigration and Ethnicity in the 1980s*, Longman Cheshire, Melbourne, 1985, 242.

35   K Rivett, 'Refugees', in J Jupp (ed.), *The Australian People: An encyclopedia of the nation, its people and their origins,* Cambridge University Press, Cambridge, 2001, 831–832.

36   Jupp, *From White Australia to Woomera*, 13; *The Politics of Australian Immigration*; S Brawley, 'Slaying the White Australia dragon: Some factors in the abolition of the White Australia Policy', in N Viviani (ed.), *The Abolition of the White Australia Policy: The immigration reform movement revisited*, Griffith University Centre for the Study of Australia-Asia Relations, Australia-Asia Papers no. 65, June 1992, 2.

37   Australia. Department of Immigration, *The Evolution of a Policy*, Australian Government Publishing Service, Canberra, 1971, 17.

38   M Gurry and G Tavan, 'Too soft and long-haired? The Department of External Affairs and the White Australia Policy, 1946–1966', *Australian Journal of International Affairs*, 58(1), 2004, 128–129; G Tavan, 'The dismantling of the White Australia Policy: Elite conspiracy or will of the people?', *Australian Journal of Political Science*, 39(1), 2004, 116.

39   EG Whitlam, Australia, *Commonwealth Parliamentary Debates*, House of Representatives, 24 May 1973, 2644–2645, 2649.

40   See further: NHC Nguyen, 'Memory in the aftermath of war: Australian responses to the Vietnamese refugee crisis of 1975', *Canadian Journal of Law and Society*, 30(2), 2015, 183–201.

41   A Jordens, *Alien to Citizen: Settling migrants in Australia, 1945–75*, Allen & Unwin, Sydney, 1997, 18–19, 226; N Viviani and J Lawe-Davies, *Australian Government Policy on the Entry of Vietnamese Refugees, 1976 to 1978*, Research Paper no. 2, Centre for the Study of Australian-Asian Relations, Griffith University, 1980, 2.

42   G Tavan, 'Immigration: Control or colour bar? The immigration reform movement, 1959–1966', *Australian Historical Studies*, 112, 2001, 195.

43   K Rivett, 'The immigration reform movement', in Viviani (ed.), *The Abolition of the White Australia Policy*, 16.

44   Rivett, 'The immigration reform movement', 15. See also: Hawkins, *Critical Years in Immigration*, 103.

45   G Tavan, *The Long, Slow Death of White Australia*, Scribe Publications, Melbourne, 2005, 205; Jupp, *From White Australia to Woomera*, 42; Viviani, *The Long Journey*, 109.

46   Viviani, *The Indochinese in Australia, 1975 to 1995*, 159; MV Tran, 'Vietnamese refugees in Australia', in J Jupp (ed.), *The Australian People*, 722; C Stevens, 'Cambodians (Khmer)', in Jupp (ed.), *The Australian People*, 191, 857; T Phoumirath, 'Laotians', in Jupp (ed.), *The Australian People*, 551.

47   UN General Assembly, Protocol Relating to the Status of Refugees, 31 January 1967, 606 UNTS 267.

48   K Neumann, *Across the Seas: Australia's response to refugees: A history*, Black Inc., Melbourne, 2015, 144–182.

49   A Bauman, oral history with interviewer K Saul, United States District Court Historical Society, Oregon, 21 November 2005, transcript, 267.

50   Australia. Senate Standing Committee on Foreign Affairs and Defence, 'Australia and the Refugee Problem', 24.

51 Australia. Senate Standing Committee on Foreign Affairs and Defence, 'Australia and the Refugee Problem', 89.

52 Australia. The Liberal and National Country Parties, *Immigration and Ethnic Affairs Policy*, August 1975.

53 M MacKellar, Australia, *Commonwealth Parliamentary Debates*, House of Representatives, 24 May 1977, 1713–1716.

54 GS Goodwin-Gill, 'The refugee situation today' in CA Price (ed.), *Refugees: The challenge of the future*, Academy of the Social Sciences in Australia, Fourth Academy Symposium, 3–4 November 1980, Academy of the Social Sciences in Australia, Canberra, 1981, 17.

55 See further: GJL Coles, 'Temporary refuge and the large scale influx of refugees'. *Australian Yearbook of International Law*, 8, 1983, 189–212.

56 N Viviani, in Price (ed.), *Refugees: The challenge of the future*, 104.

1 Controlling the story

1   R Sutton, 'Anniversary of first Vietnam boat marked', SBS, 27 April 2011, <www.sbs.com.au/news/article/2011/04/27/anniversary-first-vietnam-boat-marked>, accessed 28 May 2017. See also: MV Tran, *The Long Journey: Australia's first boatpeople*, Research Paper no. 15, Centre for the Study of Australian-Asian Relations, Griffith University, 1981, 10–11.

2   See further: Australia. Senate Standing Committee on Foreign Affairs and Defence, Reference: South-Vietnamese Refugees, Hansard, Australian Government Publishing Service, Canberra, 1976, 847; Australia. Senate Standing Committee on Foreign Affairs and Defence, 'Australia and the Refugee Problem', 46–48.

3   Australia. Senate Standing Committee on Foreign Affairs and Defence, 'Australia and the Refugee Problem', 76.

4   Australia. Senate Standing Committee on Foreign Affairs and Defence, Reference: South Vietnamese, Hansard, 'Profile of persons selected in Hong Kong, Singapore and Malaysia', 17 October 1975, 513–514.

5   Viviani and Lawe-Davies, *Australian Government Policy on the Entry of Vietnamese Refugees, 1976 to 1978*, 4; Neumann, 'Oblivious to the obvious? Australian asylum-seeker policies and the use of the past', 56.

6   Tran, *The Long Journey*, 1, 13; 'South Vietnamese refugees arrive in Darwin', the *Canberra Times*, 29 April 1976, 10.

7   Interview with W Gibbons, 9 July 2011, Oxford (transcript with author).

8   'Vietnamese refugees', 12 November 1975, NAA A1209 1975/1502.

9   'Contingency planning for unauthorised arrival of Vietnamese refugees', 19 May 1975, NAA A1209 1975/1689.

10 Notes on Cabinet Submission 192, 19 May 1966, NAA A5841 207.

11 Interview with W Gibbons.

12 Goodwin-Gill Collection, Bodleian Social Science Library, University of Oxford (hereafter Goodwin-Gill Collection), DORS Minutes, Note for File: concerning visit to Darwin 18 to 21 April 1979.

13   Jupp, *From White Australia to Woomera*, 43.
14   Australia. Department of Immigration and Ethnic Affairs, *Review '76*,
      Australian Government Publishing Service, Canberra, 6.
15   Australia. Department of Immigration and Ethnic Affairs, *Review '76*, 28.
16   Interview with M MacKellar, 22 December 2010, Melbourne (transcript
      with author).
17   Interview with M MacKellar.
18   Hawkins, *Critical Years in Immigration*, 101.
19   Interview with M Fraser.
20   Interview with M MacKellar. See also: Various correspondence between
      M MacKellar and M Fraser, November 1977, NAA M1335 19.
21   Liberal and National Country Parties, 'Immigration and Ethnic Affairs
      Policy', August 1975, 1; Interview with M MacKellar.
22   A Moran, *The Public Life of Australian Multiculturalism*, Palgrave
      Macmillan, Cham, 2016, 31–34. See also: G Hage, 'Multiculturalism
      and white paranoia in Australia', *Journal of International Migration and
      Integration*, 3(3–4), 2002, 429.
23   Tran, *The Long Journey*, 13.
24   Tran, *The Long Journey*, 22.
25   'Vietnamese refugees offered sanctuary', *Commonwealth Record*,
      31 August 1976, 550.
26   'Vietnamese refugees accommodated in Brisbane', *Commonwealth Record*,
      12 November 1976, 1220.
27   'Vietnamese refugees to stay in Australia', *Commonwealth Record*,
      20 December 1976, 1527–28.
28   'Airlift of Vietnamese refugees', *Commonwealth Record*, 27 June 1977, 797.
29   Goodwin-Gill Collection, DORS Gen, Note for File: concerning visit
      to Darwin 18–21 April 1979; NAA A446 1981/95004 Benefits for
      unauthorised boat arrivals in Australia – Part 2; Interview with
      M MacKellar.
30   'Airlift of Vietnamese refugees', *Commonwealth Record*, 27 June 1977, 797.
31   'Warning to boat refugees', *Commonwealth Record*, 10 June 1977, 702;
      'Vietnamese boat refugees', *Commonwealth Record*, 26 June 1977, 760.
32   Viviani, *The Long Journey*, 71.
33   'Warning to boat refugees', 702.
34   'Ownership of Vietnamese refugee boat', *Commonwealth Record*,
      30 November 1977, 1792; Goodwin-Gill Collection, DORS Gen, *UNHCR
      Report on Mission to Australia from 23 November to 6 December 1977*;
      'Indochinese refugees', *Commonwealth Record*, 6 December 1977, 1850.
35   Viviani, *The Long Journey*, 1984, 70. See also: Viviani and Lawe-Davies,
      *Australian Government Policy on the Entry of Vietnamese Refugees, 1976 to
      1978*, 9.
36   K Finlay, 'The letter that saved 41 lives', *Australian Women's Weekly*,
      9 August 1978, 7.

37   GJL Coles, 'Dmitris case', 13 November 1979, NAA A1838 1634/79/2/1
      Part 1.

38   R Trood, 'Prime ministers and foreign policy', in P Weller (ed.), *Menzies
      to Keating: The development of the Australian Prime Ministership*, Hurst,
      London, 1993, 172; M Fraser, speech to Victorian State Council of
      the Liberal Party of Australia, Melbourne, 27 July 1980, published in
      Commonwealth Record, 1097–1101.

39   A Jakubowicz, 'Malcolm Fraser's life and legacy: Experts respond',
      The Conversation, 20 March 2015, <http://theconversation.com/malcolm-
      frasers-life-and-legacy-experts-respond-39111>, accessed 12 July 2017.

40   'Control over unauthorised arrivals', *Commonwealth Record*, 23 January
      1979, 64–65.

41   M MacKellar, Australia. *Commonwealth Parliamentary Debates*, House of
      Representatives, 26 May 1978, 2591.

42   Australia. Department of Immigration and Ethnic Affairs, *Review '78*, 28.

43   K Betts, 'Boatpeople and public opinion in Australia', *People and Place*,
      9(4), 2001, 40; Stevens, *Immigration policy from 1970 to the present*,
      114–115.

44   Proceedings of the Conference on the Indochina Refugee Situation held at
      the Coombs Lecture Theatre, Australian National University in Canberra,
      30–31 July 1979, audio file, National Library of Australia.

45   Goodwin-Gill Collection, AUL: Reports, *UNHCR Sydney Branch Office,
      Report for 1979 to the United Nations High Commissioner for Refugees*.

46   For example: 'Refugee resettlement program', *Commonwealth Record*,
      19 September 1977, 1269.

47   Australian Population and Immigration Council, *Immigration Policies and
      Australia's Population: A Green Paper*, Australian Government Publishing
      Service, Canberra, 1977, 42.

48   Interview with D Volker, 13 December 2011, Canberra (transcript with
      author).

49   'ACTU wants action on illegal migrants', the *Canberra Times*, 7 July 1978,
      7.

50   M MacKellar, 'Immigration principles', in Australia. *Commonwealth
      Parliamentary Debates*, House of Representatives, 7 June 1978, 3153–3160.

51   'Comments by W.A. Minister on refugees', *Commonwealth Record*,
      16–22 April 1979, 464; 'Speech to Country Liberal Party in N.T.',
      Commonwealth Record, 20 May 1978, 565.

52   See further: 'Arrival of Vietnamese refugee vessel', *Commonwealth Record*,
      25 March 1978, 267; M Cass, 'Stop this unjust queue jumping', *The
      Australian*, 29 June 1978, 7; Interview with M Cass, 21 December 2010,
      Melbourne (transcript with author).

53   Australian Labor Party National Conference, 19 July 1979, 512.

54   P Falconer, Australia. *Commonwealth Parliamentary Debates*, House of
      Representatives, 17 August 1978, 445.

55   J Jesser, 'Upsurge in race-hate campaign', the *Canberra Times*,
     21 November 1979, 23; M Liffman, 'The Wider Australian Context:
     Developing issues in ethnic affairs', supplement to *Migration Action*,
     3(2–4), Spring 1976-Autumn 1978, 12.
56   Statement by Dr Guy S Goodwin-Gill to the Australian National
     University Conference on the Indochina Refugee Situation, 30–31 July
     1979, UNHCR Branch Office for Australia and New Zealand, 15;
     Goodwin-Gill Collection, AUL: Reports, *UNHCR Sydney Branch Office,
     Report for 1979 to the United Nations High Commissioner for Refugees*.
57   Interview with M MacKellar.
58   'Boat people need humane treatment', the *Canberra Times*, 24 November
     1977, 10; R Manne, 'Indo-Chinese refugees and the Australian political
     culture', *Migration Action*, 3(2–4), Spring 1976–Autumn 1978, 11.
59   N Dibbs, 'Viet refugees now a pain in the neck', the *Straits Times*,
     29 November 1977, 12; H Kamm, 'Vietnamese influx disturbs Australia',
     the *New York Times*, 14 December 1977, 9; P Everingham, Northern
     Territory of Australia, *Parliamentary Record*, Debates, Legislative
     Assembly, 24 November 1977, 293.
60   Goodwin-Gill Collection, AUL: Reports, UNHCR Sydney Branch
     Office, *Report to the United Nations High Commissioner for Refugees
     January–December 1977*; AD Lawrie, Northern Territory of Australia,
     Parliamentary Record, Debates, Legislative Assembly, 23–24 November
     1977, 290–291.
61   Australian Labor Party National Conference 1979, 19 July 1979, 560.
62   F Cranston, 'Labor "might send boat refugees back"', the *Canberra Times*,
     25 November 1977, 1; Viviani, *The Long Journey*, 76; HGP Colebatch,
     'The Left re-writes its history on refugees', *Quadrant*, 54 (2010)
     <quadrant.org.au/magazine/2010/10/the-left-rewrites-its-history-on-
     refugees/>, accessed 17 March 2017.
63   AD Lawrie to P Everingham, Northern Territory of Australia,
     Parliamentary Record, Questions on Notice, Legislative Assembly,
     1 December 1977.
64   'NT head calls for Navy', the *Canberra Times*, 26 November 1977, 1.
65   'Indochinese refugees', *Commonwealth Record*, 6 December 1977, 1850;
     'Largest refugee boat nears Darwin', the *Canberra Times*, 29 November
     1977, 1; Viviani, *The Long Journey*, 75–76; K. Neumann, 'Queue-
     jumping and the perils of crossing Sydney harbour on a Manly ferry',
     Inside Story, 1 October 2014.
66   M MacKellar, 'Minister releases details of refugee arrivals', Department of
     Immigration and Ethnic Affairs, 25 November 1977.
67   MacKellar, 'Minister releases details of refugee arrivals'.
68   Viviani, *The Long Journey*, 75.
69   M MacKellar and A Peacock, 'Humanitarian issue of refugees',
     Commonwealth Record, 29 November 1977, 1792.

70 Interview with M Fraser; M Fraser and M Simons, *Malcolm Fraser: The political memoirs*, The Miegunyah Press, Melbourne, 2010, 590–592.

71 '"Stop the Refos" is the cry in Darwin', the *Canberra Times*, 1 December 1977, 1.

72 Weller, *Malcolm Fraser PM*, 368.

73 F Cranston, 'Vietnam asks for boat people', the *Canberra Times*, 1 December 1977, 1; Neumann, *Across the Seas*, 280.

74 Kamm, 'Vietnamese influx disturbs Australia'; C Cameron, *The Cameron Diaries*, Allen & Unwin, Sydney, 1990, 809.

75 'Indochinese refugees', *Commonwealth Record*, 6 December 1977, 1850.

76 Interview with D Volker.

77 'Brief for Mr D Volker – meetings with U.S. government officials, Washington – April 1978', NAA A6980 S251005 US–Australia refugee policy proposed – Washington visit – Part 1.

78 Jupp, *From White Australia to Woomera*, 181.

79 Australia. Department of Immigration and Ethnic Affairs, *Review '78*, 28.

80 Submission no 2572 Indochinese Refugees – report on visit to ASEAN capitals, August 1978, NAA A10756 LC1366 Part 1.

81 Finlay, 'The letter that saved 41 lives', 7.

82 Goodwin-Gill Collection, AUL: Reports, *UNHCR Sydney Branch Office, Report for November-December 1978*.

83 'Half of all refugees die: MacKellar', the *Canberra Times*, 23 April 1979, 10.

84 'MacKellar defends refugee policies', the *Canberra Times*, 24 September 1979, 1.

85 Australian Labor Party National Conference 1979, 19 July 1979, 513.

86 See further: Viviani, *The Long Journey*, 114; Jupp, *From White Australia to Woomera*, 125; I Macphee, Australia, *Commonwealth Parliamentary Debates,* House of Representatives, 8 May 1984, 2020.

87 J Menadue, in Price (ed.), *Refugees: The challenge of the future*, 24.

88 R Andrews, 'Refugee came to love the sea', the *Canberra Times*, 6 January 1978, 3.

89 Briefing materials, circa 17 April 1978, NAA A6980 S251019 Brief for D Volker – US-Australia refugee policy – Washington visit – April 1978 – Part 2.

90 Sutton, 'Anniversary of first Vietnam boat marked'.

91 UNHCR Regional Representation, *Human Lives, Human Rights*, November 2016, <unhcr.org.au/>, accessed 4 February 2017.

92 C Hoang (ed.), introduction to *Boatpeople: Personal stories from the Vietnamese exodus 1975–1996*, Carina Hoang Communications, Cloverdale, 2010.

93 Department of Immigration and Ethnic Affairs, *Review '86*, Australian Government Publishing Service, Canberra, 65; Viviani, *The Indochinese in Australia, 1975 to 1995*, 159; Tran, 'Vietnamese refugees in Australia', 722.

94 Tran, 'Vietnamese Refugees in Australia', 724.

95   I Macphee, 'Good vs. bad policies: The Vietnamese boat people's success story', in *Reflections on the Past, Looking to the Future*, 21st National Conference of the Vietnamese Community in Australia, Sydney, 8–10 June 2012, 45.

96   C Price, 'Immigration and Ethnic Affairs', in A Patience and B Head, *From Whitlam to Fraser: Reform and reaction in Australian politics*, Oxford University Press, Melbourne, 1979, 207–8. See further: Viviani, *The Long Journey*, 64.

97   Viviani, *The Long Journey*, 53; Stats, 'Welcome to Australia? A reappraisal of the Fraser government's approach to refugees, 1975–83', 7–10; Neumann, *Across the Seas*, 274.

98   Viviani, *The Long Journey*, 85; Australia. Senate Standing Committee on Foreign Affairs and Defence, *Indochinese Refugee Resettlement: Australia's involvement*, Australian Government Publishing Service, Canberra, 1981, 1175; Tran, 'Vietnamese refugees in Australia', 722.

99   MacKellar, Australia, *Commonwealth Parliamentary Debates*, House of Representatives, 24 May 1977, 1713–1716.

100 'Submission on Vietnamese Refugees', Australia. Senate Standing Committee on Foreign Affairs and Defence, Reference: South-Vietnamese Refugees, Hansard, 452.

101 Attachment C, Submission no 2771 Review of the Indochinese Refugee Program, November 1978, NAA LC1366 Part 2 Refugee Policy.

102 Kamm, 'Vietnamese influx disturbs Australia'.

103 Manne, 'Indo-Chinese refugees and the Australian political culture', 11.

104 AC Kevin, Notes on Submission no 2572, Indochinese Refugees – visit to ASEAN capitals, 7 September 1978, NAA A10756 LC1366 Part 1.

105 Tavan, *The Long, Slow Death of White Australia*, 214.

106 Interview with M MacKellar.

2   Recognised as refugees

1   United Nations High Commissioner for Refugees (1977), 'Determination of Refugee Status' (ExCom Conclusion No 8 (XXVIII)-1977, 12 October 1977).

2   United Nations High Commissioner for Refugees (2001) 'Global Consultations on International Protection/Third Track: Asylum Processes (Fair and Efficient Asylum Procedures)' (EC/GC/01/12, 31 May 2001) [5].

3   J McAdam and F Chong, *Why Seeking Asylum Is Legal: And Australia's policies are not*, UNSW Press, Sydney, 2014, 38.

4   'Persons in Australia who are in the process of seeking some form of asylum', undated circa 1982, NAA A1838 932/32 Part 2.

5   MacKellar, Australia, *Commonwealth Parliamentary Debates*, House of Representatives, 24 May 1977, 1713–1716.

6   'Administration of the refugee policy function', February 1983, NAA, A446 1982/95192 Part 2.

7   'Review of Australian Procedures for Determining Refugee Status', June 1983, NAA A432 1985/2834.
8   'Review of Australian Procedures for Determining Refugee Status'.
9   CL Avery, 'Refugee Status Decision-Making: The systems of ten countries', *Stanford Journal of International Law*, 19, 1983, 249.
10   Standing Committee on Refugees, Second Meeting, 20 October 1977, NAA A1838 1632/5/9/4 Part 1.
11   Standing Committee on Refugees, Sub-Committee on Australia as a Country of First Asylum – Determination of Refugee Status, Draft Report, 20 October 1977, NAA A1838 1632/5/9/4 Part 1.
12   NAA A12909 Submission No 2014: Indo-Chinese Refugees – Ongoing programme – Decision 4884(FAD).
13   Goodwin-Gill Collection, Memorandum from IC Jackson to G Jaeger, 'Report on Mission to Australia from 23 November to 6 December 1977', UNHCR, 28 December 1977.
14   Goodwin-Gill Collection, DORS Gen, *UNHCR Report on Mission to Australia from 23 November to 6 December 1977*.
15   'Vietnamese boat refugees: The dimensions of the problem for Australia', 19 December 1977, NAA A6980 S251019 Brief for D Volker – US–Australia refugee policy – Washington visit – April 1978 – Part 2.
16   Minutes of DORS meeting 3 November 1978, NAA A1838 1632/5/9/4 Part 1.
17   Goodwin-Gill Collection, DORS Gen, *UNHCR Report on Mission to Australia from 23 November to 6 December 1977*.
18   EC Irwin, 'Determination of Refugee Status Committee', 7 February 1978, NAA A1838 1632/5/9/4 Part 1.
19   MacKellar, Australia, *Commonwealth Parliamentary Debates*, House of Representatives, 24 May 1977, 1713-1716; J McAdam, 'From Humanitarian Discretion to Complementary Protection: Reflections on the emergence of human rights-based refugee protection in Australia', *Australian International Law Journal*, 18, 2011, 53–76.
20   M Crock, 'Judging refugees: The clash of power and institutions in the development of Australian refugee law', *Sydney Law Review*, 26, 2004, 54.
21   MacKellar, Australia, *Commonwealth Parliamentary Debates*, House of Representatives, 24 May 1977, 1713–1716.
22   M MacKellar, Australia, *Commonwealth Parliamentary Debates*, House of Representatives, 21 August 1979, 373; Goodwin-Gill Collection, DORS Gen, Telex, 8 June 1979.
23   See further: M MacKellar, Australia. *Commonwealth Parliamentary Debates*, House of Representatives, 22 August 1978, 590.
24   York, 'The myth of our humanitarian tradition'; Viviani, *The Long Journey*, 80; Stevens, *Immigration policy from 1970 to the present*, 111.
25   United Nations High Commissioner for Refugees (1977), 'Determination of Refugee Status'; See also: GS Goodwin-Gill and J McAdam, *The*

Refugee in International Law, Oxford University Press, Oxford, 2006, 529–530.
26   AR Greville, Department of Prime Minister and Cabinet, 'Determination of refugee status mechanism', 16 June 1982, in NAA A1209 1987/150 Part 1.
27   Submission no. 1916 Indochinese Refugees, February 1978, NAA, A12909 1916.
28   M MacKellar, 'Speech to Institute of International Affairs', *Commonwealth Record,* 19 August 1978, 1066.
29   MacKellar, 'Speech to Institute of International Affairs'.
30   A Clark, 'The boat people force a policy turnabout', the *National Times*, week ending 13 May 1978, in Goodwin-Gill Collection, DORS Gen.
31   Goodwin-Gill Collection, DORS Gen, Note for File 9 November 1978.
32   Goodwin-Gill Collection, DORS Gen, 'Crew members – Con Dao 3', s29 August 1979; Goodwin-Gill Collection, untitled report, UNHCR Sydney Branch Office, 9 October 1978, DORS Gen.
33   Goodwin-Gill Collection, DORS Minutes, Note for File: concerning meeting on 9 November 1978.
34   Goodwin-Gill Collection, DORS Minutes, *UNHCR, Report from the Legal Consultant, UNHCR Sydney, on the DORS Committee Meeting of 15 August 1978.*
35   Goodwin-Gill Collection, G Rizzo, untitled report, UNHCR Sydney Branch Office, 9 October 1978, DORS Gen.
36   Goodwin-Gill Collection, untitled report, UNHCR Sydney Branch Office, 9 October 1978, DORS Gen.
37   Goodwin-Gill Collection, DORS Minutes, Note for File: concerning meeting on 10 October 1978.
38   Goodwin-Gill Collection, DORS Minutes, Note for File: concerning meeting on 10 October 1978.
39   Minutes of DORS meeting 3 November 1978, NAA A1838 1632/5/9/4 Part 1.
40   Goodwin-Gill Collection, DORS Minutes, Note for File: concerning meeting on 10 October 1978.
41   Goodwin-Gill Collection, DORS Minutes, Note for File: concerning meeting on 10 October 1978.
42   Minutes of DORS meeting, 3 November 1978, NAA A1838 1632/5/9/4 Part 1.
43   Goodwin-Gill Collection, DORS Minutes, Note for File: concerning meeting of 3 November 1978.
44   Goodwin-Gill Collection, DORS Minutes, Note for File: concerning meeting on 3 November 1978.
45   Goodwin-Gill Collection, DORS Minutes, Note for File: concerning meeting on 15 March 1979; Goodwin-Gill Collection, DORS Minutes, Note for File: concerning meeting on 26 April 1979.

46   Goodwin-Gill Collection, DORS Minutes, Note for File: concerning meeting on 26 April 1979.

47   Goodwin-Gill Collection, DORS Minutes, Note for File: concerning meeting on 26 April 1979.

48   Goodwin-Gill Collection, DORS Gen, *UNHCR, Report on visit to the Department of Foreign Affairs and the Department of Immigration and Ethnic Affairs, Canberra, on 14 November 1978.*

49   See further: C Higgins, 'New evidence on refugee status determination in Australia, 1978 to 1983', *Refugee Survey Quarterly*, 35(3), 2016, 71–93; Goodwin-Gill Collection, AUL: Reports, *UNHCR Sydney Branch Office, Report for 1982 to the United Nations High Commissioner for Refugees*; 'Review of Australian procedures for determining refugee status', June 1983, NAA A432 1985/2834.

50   Avery, 'Refugee status decision-making', 352.

51   Submission no. 2771 Review of the Indo-Chinese Refugee Program, November 1978, NAA, A12909 2771.

52   Fraser and Simons, *Malcolm Fraser: The political memoirs*, 419; Submission no. 2771 Review of the Indo-Chinese Refugee Program, November 1978, NAA A10756 LC1366 Part 2.

53   See further: Goodwin-Gill Collection, DORS Minutes, October 1978–April 1983.

54   Goodwin-Gill Collection, DORS Minutes, Note for File: concerning meeting on 6 December 1978; Goodwin-Gill Collection, DORS Minutes, Note for File: concerning meeting on 15 March 1979.

55   Goodwin-Gill Collection, DORS Minutes, Note for File: concerning meeting on 26 April 1979.

56   Goodwin-Gill Collection, DORS Minutes, Note for File: dated 6 December 1978.

57   Goodwin-Gill Collection, DORS Minutes, Note for File: dated 6 December 1978.

58   Goodwin-Gill Collection, AUL: Reports, *UNHCR Sydney Branch Office, Report to the United Nations High Commissioner for Refugees for 1978.*

59   Goodwin-Gill Collection, DORS Minutes, Note for File: concerning meeting on 22 February 1979; Goodwin-Gill Collection, DORS Minutes, Note for File: concerning meeting on 26 April 1979.

60   Goodwin-Gill Collection, DORS Minutes, Note for File: concerning meeting on 9 January 1979.

61   Goodwin-Gill Collection, DORS Minutes, Note for File: concerning meeting on 22 November 1978.

62   Goodwin-Gill, DORS Minutes, Note for File: concerning meeting on 26 April 1979.

63   Goodwin-Gill Collection, DORS Minutes, Note for File: concerning meeting on 9 January 1979.

64 Goodwin-Gill Collection, DORS Minutes, Note for File: concerning meeting on 15 March 1979.

65 Goodwin-Gill Collection, DORS Minutes, Note for File: concerning meeting on 15 March 1979.

66 Goodwin-Gill Collection, DORS Minutes, Note for File: concerning meeting on 21 March 1979.

67 Goodwin-Gill Collection, DORS Minutes, Note for File: concerning meeting on 21 March 1979.

68 Goodwin-Gill Collection, DORS Minutes, Note for File: concerning meeting on 15 March 1979.

69 Goodwin-Gill Collection, DORS Minutes, Note for File: concerning meeting on 21 March 1979.

70 See further: Higgins, 'New evidence on refugee status determination in Australia, 1978 to 1983', 71–93. Of 409 decisions, Immigration's opinion on an applicant is listed 24 per cent of the time; Foreign Affairs 44 per cent; Attorney-General's 23 per cent; Prime Minister and Cabinet 26 per cent; and UNHCR 34 per cent.

71 Goodwin-Gill Collection, DORS Minutes, Note for File: concerning meeting on 1 May 1980.

72 Goodwin-Gill Collection, DORS Minutes, Note for File: concerning meeting on 1 May 1980.

73 Goodwin-Gill Collection, DORS Minutes, Note for File: concerning meeting on 26 April 1979.

74 Goodwin-Gill Collection, DORS Minutes, Note for File: concerning meeting on 21 March 1979.

75 Higgins, 'New evidence on refugee status determination in Australia, 1978 to 1983', 71–93.

76 Goodwin-Gill Collection, DORS Minutes, Note for File: concerning meeting on 26 April 1979.

77 Goodwin-Gill Collection, DORS Minutes, Note for File: concerning meeting on 16 October 1979.

78 Goodwin-Gill Collection, DORS Minutes, Note for File: concerning DORS procedural meeting on 9 July 1980.

79 'Persons in Australia who are in the process of seeking some form of asylum; Attachment A', in NAA A1838 932/32 Part 2; Goodwin-Gill Collection, AUL: Reports, *UNHCR Sydney Branch Office, Report for 1980 to the United Nations High Commissioner for Refugees*; Goodwin-Gill Collection, DORS Minutes, Note for File: concerning meeting on 6 August 1980.

80 'Persons in Australia who are in the process of seeking some form of asylum; Attachment A'.

81 Goodwin-Gill Collection, DORS Minutes, Note for File: concerning DORS procedural meeting on 9 July 1980.

82 Goodwin-Gill Collection, DORS Minutes, Note for File: concerning DORS procedural meeting on 9 July 1980.

3 A country of resettlement

1   Briefing materials circa 17 April 1978, NAA A6980 S251019 Brief for
    D Volker – US–Australia refugee policy – Washington visit – April 1978 –
    Part 2.
2   'Intake figures' in briefing materials circa 17 April 1978, NAA A6980
    S251019 Brief for D Volker – US–Australia refugee policy – Washington
    visit – April 1978 – Part 2.
3   D Volker, 'Indochinese refugees – discussions in Washington 26–27 April
    1978 – points of agreement', 2 May 1978, NAA A6980 S251020 US–
    Australia refugee policy proposed – Washington visit – Part 3.
4   L Engledow to M MacKellar, 'Boat refugees – alternative policy options',
    circa April 1978, NAA A6980 S251020 US–Australia refugee policy
    proposed – Washington visit – Part 3.
5   'Refugee team for Thailand', *Commonwealth Record*, 26 July 1977, 956;
    'Intake figures' in briefing materials circa 17 April 1978, NAA A6980
    S251019 Brief for D Volker – US–Australia refugee policy – Washington
    visit – April 1978 – Part 2.
6   'Summary of small boat arrivals', circa April 1978, NAA A6980 S251019
    Brief for D Volker – US–Australia refugee policy – Washington visit –
    April 1978 – Part 2.
7   'Summary of small boat arrivals'.
8   T Lewis, *Wrecks in Darwin waters*, Turton and Armstrong, Wahroonga
    NSW, 1992, 78; Australian Royal Commission of Inquiry into Drugs,
    Report: Book B: Parts VI–IX, Australian Government Publishing Service,
    Canberra, 1980, B357.
9   Interview with D Volker.
10 Goodwin-Gill Collection, AUL: Reports, UNHCR Sydney Branch Office,
    *Report to the United Nations High Commissioner for Refugees January–
    December 1977*.
11 P Everingham, Northern Territory of Australia, Parliamentary Record,
    Questions Without Notice, Legislative Assembly, 22 May 1979, 610.
12 'Brief for Mr D Volker – meetings with U.S. government officials,
    Washington – April 1978', NAA A6980 S251005 US–Australia refugee
    policy proposed – Washington visit – Part 1.
13 'Vietnamese boat refugees: The dimensions of the problem for Australia',
    19 December 1977, NAA A6980 S251019 Brief for D Volker – US–
    Australia refugee policy – Washington visit – April 1978 – Part 2; Australia.
    Department of Immigration and Ethnic Affairs, *Review '78*, 28.
14 'Brief for Mr D Volker – meetings with U.S. government officials,
    Washington – April 1978', NAA A6980 S251005 US–Australia refugee
    policy proposed – Washington visit – Part 1.
15 'Vietnamese boat refugees', Joint Intelligence Organisation, Office of Current
    Intellligence, 23 January 1978, NAA A6980 S251019 Brief for D Volker –
    US–Australia refugee policy – Washington visit – April 1978 – Part 2.

16   United Nations General Assembly Official Records: Thirty-third Session, *Report of the United Nations High Commissioner for Refugees, Supplement No.12 (A/33/12)*, 12 September 1978.

17   'Vietnamese boat refugees', Joint Intelligence Organisation, Office of Current Intelligence, 23 January 1978.

18   'Vietnamese boat refugees', Joint Intelligence Organisation, Office of Current Intellligence, 23 January 1978.

19   'Brief for Mr D Volker – meetings with U.S. government officials, Washington – April 1978', NAA A6980 S251005 US–Australia refugee policy proposed – Washington visit – Part 1.

20   H Kamm, 'Vietnam is acting to halt escapes', the *New York Times*, 30 December 1977, 1.

21   'Vietnamese boat refugees: Dimensions of the problem for Australia'.

22   'Vietnamese boat refugees: Dimensions of the problem for Australia'.

23   E Moloney, Interview with AM Jordens, Chief Migration Officers Oral History Project, National Library of Australia, 20 May 2008.

24   WC Robinson, *Terms of Refuge*, Zed Books, London, 1988, 26–28; H Kamm, 'Refugees tell of the hardships and fear they say drove them from Vietnam', the *New York Times*, 20 September 1977, 3.

25   L Engledow to M MacKellar, 'Boat refugees – alternative policy options'. See further: Viviani, *The Long Journey*, 42; Hawkins, *Critical Years in Immigration*, 179–182.

26   Submission no. 2173 Indochinese Refugees Programme for 1978/79, May 1978, NAA A10756 LC1366 – Part 1. See also: Proceedings of the Conference on the Indochina Refugee Situation.

27   Submission no. 2173 Indochinese Refugees Programme for 1978/79, May 1978.

28   'Arrival of Vietnamese refugee vessel', *Commonwealth Record*, 25 March 1978, 267.

29   'More lurid: MacKellar', the *Canberra Times*, 28 March 1978, 3.

30   'Refugees genuine, officials believe', the *Canberra Times*, 28 March 1978, 3.

31   'Boat people arriving in Australia who have been approved for entry to the USA', April 1978, NAA A6980 S251005 US–Australia refugee policy proposed – Washington visit – Part 1.

32   L Engledow to M MacKellar, 'Boat refugees – alternative policy options'.

33   L Engledow to M MacKellar, 'Boat refugees – alternative policy options'.

34   L Engledow to M MacKellar, 28 April 1978, NAA A6980 S251020 US–Australia refugee policy proposed – Washington visit – Part 3.

35   A Weatherstone to M Liveris, 'Hai Hong Refugee Boat', 8 November 1978, NAA A6980 S251099 Part 1; N Hoffmann, interview with AM Jordens, National Library of Australia, Chief Migration Officers Oral History Project, 15 April 2008, transcript, 40–41.

36   R Eckersley, 'Malcolm Fraser: "We have lost our way"', the *Conversation*, 10 October 2011, <theconversation.com/malcolm-fraser-we-have-lost-our-way-3734>, accessed 12 July 2017.

37　Interview with M Fraser.

38　Hawkins, *Critical Years in Immigration*, 120.

39　L Engledow to M MacKellar, 28 April 1978.

40　I Simington to M Fraser, 22 March 1978, NAA A10756 LC1366 – Part 1.

41　Hoffmann, 37.

42　C Hogue to I Macphee, 6 April 1982, A446 1982/95101 Possible refugee situation – Falkland Islands.

43　A Dastyari, *United States Migrant Interdiction and the Detention of Refugees at Guantanamo Bay*, Cambridge University Press, New York, 2015, 13.

44　United Nations General Assembly Official Records: Thirty-ninth Session, *Report of the United Nations High Commissioner for Refugees Supplement No. 12 (A/39/12)*, 24 August 1984.

45　M MacKellar to M Fraser, 17 February 1978, NAA A10756 LC1366 Part 1.

46　Viviani, *The Long Journey*, 80.

47　Australia. Department of Immigration and Ethnic Affairs, *Review '79*, Australian Government Publishing Service, Canberra, 14.

48　'Brief for Mr D Volker – meetings with U.S. government officials, Washington – April 1978', NAA A6980 S251005 US–Australia refugee policy proposed – Washington visit – Part 1.

49　A Clark, 'The boat people force a policy turnabout', the *National Times*, week ending 13 May 1978, 9, in Goodwin-Gill Collection.

50　B Gwertzman, 'White House urged to authorise entry of 15,000 Indochinese', the *New York Times*, 4 July 1977, 1.

51　'Singapore, already crowded, further tightens stringent policy restricting refugees from Indochina', the *New York Times*, 12 November 1978, 6; B Wain, *The Refused: The agony of the Indochina refugees*, Simon & Schuster, New York, 1981, 200; Australia. Senate Standing Committee on Foreign Affairs and Defence, *Indochinese Refugee Resettlement: Australia's Involvement*, 1165.

52　'Singapore, already crowded, further tightens stringent policy restricting refugees from Indochina', the *New York Times*; H Kamm, 'Singapore is a bitter harbour for Vietnamese refugees', the *New York Times*, 13 June 1977, 16.

53　K St Cartmail, *Exodus Indochina*, Heinemann, Auckland, 1983, 214; L Clinton Thompson, *Refugee Workers in the Indochina Exodus, 1975 to 1982*, McFarland and Co., Jefferson, 2010, 175–177; Robinson, *Terms of Refuge*, 46–49.

54　Proceedings of the Conference on the Indochina Refugee Situation, 30–31 July 1979, audio file.

55　Statement by Dr Guy S Goodwin-Gill to the Australian National University Conference on the Indochina Refugee Situation, 15.

56　H Kamm, 'New hurdles for Vietnam "boat people"', the *New York Times*, 5 December 1977, 39; NAA A6980 S251019 Brief for D Volker – US–Australia refugee policy – Washington visit – April 1978 – Part 2.

57　'Refugee policies of other governments', circa March/April 1978, attachment to 'Brief for Mr D Volker – meetings with U.S. government

officials, Washington – April 1978', NAA A6980 S251019 Brief for
D Volker – US–Australia refugee policy – Washington visit – April 1978 –
Part 2.

58   Robinson, *Terms of Refuge*, 23; United Nations General Assembly
Official Records: Thirty-first Session, *Report of the United Nations High
Commissioner for Refugees, Supplement No. 12 (A/31/12)*, 1 January 1976.

59   United Nations High Commissioner for Refugees, *Award Statement
by Prince Sadruddin Aga Khan, United Nations High Commissioner for
Refugees, on the occasion of the award of the Nansen Medal for 1977 to
the Malaysian Red Crescent Society, Geneva*, 10 October 1977, <www.
unhcr.org/en-au/admin/hcspeeches/3ae68fc014/award-statement-prince-
sadruddin-aga-khan-united-nations-high-commissioner.html>, accessed
25 February 2017.

60   Submission no. 2771 Review of the Indo-Chinese Refugee Program,
November 1978, NAA A12909 2771; Wain, *The Refused*, 130–135.

61   'Vietnamese boat refugees: the dimensions of the problem for Australia'.

62   Submission no. 2771 Review of the Indo-Chinese Refugee Program,
November 1978, NAA A12909 2771.

63   Cartmail, *Exodus Indochina*, 222–223.

64   Robinson, *Terms of Refuge*, 60.

65   D Lee, 'My mother', in C Hoang (ed.), *Boat People: Personal stories
from the Vietnamese exodus 1975–1996*, 56; C Luu, 'Boat HG3438',
in C Hoang (ed.), *Boat People*, 71.

66   D Volker, 'Indochinese refugees – discussions in Washington 26–27 April
1978 – points of agreement', 2 May 1978, NAA A6980 S251020 Brief
for D Volker – US–Australia refugee policy – Washington visit –April
1978 – Part 3.

67   'Brief for Mr D Volker – meetings with US government officials,
Washington – April 1978', NAA A6980 S251005 US–Australia refugee
policy proposed – Washington visit – Part 1.

68   D Volker, 'Indochinese refugees – discussions in Washington 26–27 April
1978 – points of agreement'.

69   D Volker, 'Indochinese refugees – discussions in Washington 26–27 April
1978 – points of agreement'.

70   D Volker, 'Indochinese refugees – discussions in Washington 26–27 April
1978 – points of agreement'.

71   G Humphries, quoted in H Martin, *Angels and Arrogant Gods*, Australian
Government Publishing Service, Canberra, 1989, 107. See also: W
Gibbons, 'The boats were not sabotaged', *Pearls and Irritations*, 21 March
2014, <http://johnmenadue.com/wayne-gibbons-the-boats-were-not-
sabotaged>, accessed 12 July 2017.

72   T Barshall, 'Compassion fatigue', in Hoang (ed.), *Boat People*, 22–28;
Martin, *Angels and Arrogant Gods*, 103–107.

73   W Gibbons quoted in Martin, *Angels and Arrogant Gods*, 103–104.

74 Submission no. 2771 Review of the Indo-Chinese Refugee Program, November 1978, NAA A12909 2771.

75 Cartmail, *Exodus Indochina*, 213; H Pham and K Pham, 'Vietnamese chicken glass noodle soup, and a family story', *Christian Science Monitor*, 2 May 2013, <www.csmonitor.com/The-Culture/Food/Stir-It-Up/2013/0502/Vietnamese-chicken-glass-noodle-soup-and-a-family-story>, accessed 12 March 2017; R Yates, 'Freedoms "slipping away"', *Chicago Tribune*, 11 September 1978, 4.

76 K Finlay, 'Michael MacKellar's heartbreak job', the *Australian Women's Weekly*, 16 August 1978, 17.

77 L Engledow to M MacKellar, 'Boat refugees – alternative policy options'.

78 '38 refugees at Darwin', the *Canberra Times*, 14 November 1978, 3.

79 Goodwin-Gill Collection, AUL: Reports, *UNHCR Sydney Branch Office, Report for 1978*.

80 Submission no. 2771 Review of the Indo-Chinese Refugee Program, November 1978, NAA A12909 2771.

81 Viviani, *The Long Journey*, 84; interview with M Fraser; interview with M MacKellar.

82 Minister for Immigration and Ethnic Affairs, 'Refugees from Vietnam', press release, 4 January 1979; Robinson, *Terms of Refuge*, 30–31.

83 Wain, *The Refused*, 110.

84 Goodwin-Gill Collection, AUL: Reports, *UNHCR Sydney Branch Office, Report for January 1979*; Robinson, *Terms of Refuge*, 28–29, 138; H Adelman, *Canada and the Indochinese Refugees*, LA Weigl Educational Associates, Regina, 1982, 35.

85 Goodwin-Gill Collection, DORS Gen, *UNHCR Report on visit to the Department of Foreign Affairs and the Department of Immigration and Ethnic Affairs, Canberra, on 14 November 1978*.

86 B Gwertzman, 'Indochina refugee crisis causes US policy review', the *New York Times*, 15 November 1978, 1; H Kamm, 'A confrontation on refugees', the *New York Times*, 28 June 1979, 4; Wain, *The Refused*, 112–122; '8 in Hong Kong trial accused of smuggling people from Vietnam', the *New York Times*, 8 June 1979, 11.

87 US Embassy Canberra, telegram, 'Indochinese refugees: A new approach required', 16 November 1978, NAA A6980 S251099 Part 1.

88 Submission no. 2771 Review of the Indo-Chinese Refugee Program, November 1978, NAA A12909 2771.

89 Memorandum no. 380 'Indo Chinese Refugees', 11 July 1979, NAA A12390 380.

90 Submission no. 2771 Review of the Indo-Chinese Refugee Program, November 1978, NAA A12909 2771.

91 H Kamm, 'Indochina refugee parlay opens', the *New York Times*, 12 December 1978, 4; Minister for Immigration and Ethnic Affairs, *Text of a statement by the Minister for Immigration and Ethnic Affairs,*

the Hon. MJR Mackellar, Delivered to the UNHCR consultative meeting on the Indo-Chinese refugee situation at Geneva, press release, 11 December 1978.

92 US Embassy Canberra, telegram, 'Indochinese refugees: A new approach required', 16 November 1978, NAA A6980 S251099 Part 1.

93 AJ Ayers, Notes on Cabinet Submission no. 2771 Review of the Indochinese refugee programme, 24 November 1978, NAA A10756 LC1366 Part 2.

94 US Embassy Canberra, telegram, 'Indochinese refugees: A new approach required', 16 November 1978, NAA A6980 S251099 Part 1.

4   A country of 'first asylum'

1 'Humanitarian issue of refugees', *Commonwealth Record*, 29 November 1977, 1792.

2 M Mackellar, 'Speech to Institute of International Affairs', *Commonwealth Record*, 19 August 1978, 1066.

3 Submission no. 2173 Indochinese Refugees: Programme for 1978/79, May 1978, NAA A10756 LC1366 Part 1.

4 D Volker, 'Indochinese Refugees – discussions in Washington 26–27 April 1978 – points of agreement'.

5 'Vietnamese boat refugees: The dimensions of the problem for Australia'.

6 Goodwin-Gill Collection, DORS Minutes, Note for File: concerning meeting on 3 November 1978.

7 Wain, *The Refused*, 16–35. See also: Viviani, *The Long Journey*, 85–87.

8 Goodwin-Gill Collection, DORS Minutes, Note for File: concerning meeting on 3 November 1978; Goodwin-Gill Collection, DORS Minutes, Note for File: concerning meeting on 10 October 1978.

9 I Simington to L Engledow, undated circa 2 November 1978, NAA A6980 S251099 Part 1.

10 Wain, *The Refused*, 27.

11 '143 feared lost as refugee boat sinks off Malaysia', the *New York Times*, 3 December 1978, 19.

12 Wain, *The Refused*, 27; 'Reports on Vietnamese refugee boat', *Commonwealth Record*, 6 November 1978, 1547.

13 Opening Statement by Mr Poul Hartling, United Nations High Commissioner for Refugees, at the Consultative Meeting with Interested Governments on Refugees and Displaced Persons in South-East Asia, Geneva, 11 December 1978.

14 Goodwin-Gill Collection, DORS Gen, *UNHCR Report on visit to the Department of Foreign Affairs and the Department of Immigration and Ethnic Affairs, Canberra, on 14 November 1978*.

15 Goodwin-Gill Collection, DORS Gen, *UNHCR Report on visit to the Department of Foreign Affairs and the Department of Immigration and Ethnic Affairs, Canberra, on 14 November 1978*.

16   Goodwin-Gill Collection, DORS Gen, *UNHCR Report on visit to the Department of Foreign Affairs and the Department of Immigration and Ethnic Affairs, Canberra, on 14 November 1978.*

17   JA Nimmo to I Simington, undated, circa 9 November 1978, 'Interception – Unauthorised large vessel arrivals (particular reference to *Hai Hong*)', Attachment A: minutes of meeting 9 November 1978, NAA A6980 S251099 Part 1.

18   JA Nimmo to I Simington.

19   Submission no. 2906, Review of Indochinese Refugee Situation, Decision no. 7510, January 1979, NAA A12909 2906.

20   Decision no. 7510, Submission no. 2906, Review of Indochinese Refugee Situation, 23 January 1979, NAA A10756 LC1366 Part 2.

21   Trood, 'Prime ministers and foreign policy', 173.

22   Goodwin-Gill Collection, DORS Minutes, Note for File: concerning meeting 9 January 1979.

23   Hoffmann, 37, 41–42, 49; 'Refugees genuine, officials believe', the *Canberra Times*, 28 March 1978, 3.

24   Submission no. 2906, Review of Indochinese Refugee Situation, January 1979, NAA A10756 LC1366 Part 2.

25   KS Hutchings, Notes on Cabinet Submission no. 2906, Review of Indochinese Refugee Situation, 19 January 1979, NAA A10756 LC1366 Part 2.

26   D Marr and M Wilkinson, *Dark Victory*, Allen & Unwin, Sydney, 2003.

27   Decision no. 7510, Submission no. 2906, Review of Indochinese Refugee Situation, 23 January 1979, NAA A10756 LC1366 Part 2.

28   Submission no. 2906, Review of Indochinese Refugee Situation, January 1979, NAA A10756 LC1366 Part 2.

29   R Manne, 'How we came to be so cruel to asylum seekers', the *Conversation*, 26 October 2016, <theconversation.com/robert-manne-how-we-came-to-be-so-cruel-to-asylum-seekers-67542>, accessed 18 April 2017.

30   Submission no. 2906, Review of Indochinese Refugee Situation, January 1979, NAA A10756 LC1366 Part 2.

31   M Crock and K Bones, 'Australian Exceptionalism: Temporary protection and the rights of refugees', *Melbourne Journal of International Law*, 16, 2016, 2–3.

32   Jean Francois Durieux and Jane McAdam write that 'the Convention architecture is itself characterised by a gradual improvement of standards of treatment over time' – see further: JF Durieux and J McAdam, '*Non-refoulement* through time: The case for a derogation clause to the Refugee Convention in mass influx emergencies', *International Journal of Refugee Law*, 16(1), 2004, 14.

33   Submission no. 3200, Legislation Against Unauthorised Boat Arrivals, NAA A10765 LC1366 Part 2.

34   Submission no. 3200, Legislation Against Unauthorised Boat Arrivals, 25 May 1979, NAA A10756 LC1366 Part 2; Decision no. 7510,

Submission no. 2906, Review of Indochinese Refugee Situation, 23 January 1979, NAA A10756 LC1366 Part 2.

35   Decision no. 8905, 7 June 1979, Submission no. 3200: Legislation against unauthorised boat arrivals, NAA A12909 3200.

36   CD Samuel to N Hoffmann, Legislation Against Unauthorised Boat Arrivals, 24 May 1979, NAA A10756 LC1366 Part 2.

37   Australian Labor Party National Conference, 19 July 1979, 514.

38   Goodwin-Gill Collection, DORS Minutes, Note for File: concerning discussion on 9 May 1979.

39   Goodwin-Gill Collection, DORS Minutes, Note for File: concerning discussion on 9 May 1979.

40   Goodwin-Gill Collection, DORS Minutes, Note for File: concerning discussion on 9 May 1979.

41   Goodwin-Gill Collection, DORS Minutes, Note for File: concerning discussion on 9 May 1979.

42   Goodwin-Gill Collection, DORS Minutes, Note for File: concerning discussion on 9 May 1979.

43   Goodwin-Gill Collection, DORS Minutes, Note for File: concerning discussion on 9 January 1979.

44   'Humanitarian issue of refugees', *Commonwealth Record*, 29 November 1977, 1792; 'Comments by WA Minister on refugees', 464; M Mackellar, 'Speech to Commonwealth Club of Adelaide', *Commonwealth Record*, 26 April 1979, 500; M Mackellar, 'Speech to National Press Club', *Commonwealth Record*, 15 August 1979, 1154.

45   In May 1978 MacKellar told Parliament that six crew members of the *Song Be 12* chose to remain onboard and return to Vietnam. He also stated that one person had returned to Indonesia from a boat that arrived in March 1978 via Jakarta. See further: Viviani, *The Long Journey*, 77; M MacKellar, Australia. *Commonwealth Parliamentary Debates,* House of Representatives, 9 May 1978, 2096.

46   Memorandum no. 380, Indochinese Refugees, 11 July 1979.

47   Memorandum no. 380, Indochinese Refugees, 11 July 1979.

48   Memorandum no. 380, Indochinese Refugees, 11 July 1979.

49   GLJ Coles, 'Dmitris case', 13 November 1979, NAA A1838 1634/79/2/1 Part 1.

50   UN General Assembly, *Meeting on Refugees and Displaced Persons in South-East Asia, convened by the Secretary-General of the United Nations at Geneva, on 20 and 21 July 1979 and subsequent developments: Report of the Secretary-General,* 7 November 1979, A/34/627.

51   L Thomson, 'Indochinese refugees: Geneva meeting: second discussion at US embassy', 11 July 1979, and 'Indochinese refugees: international meeting: discussion at US embassy', 4 July 1979, NAA A432 E1977/6390 Part 2.

52   'Indochinese refugees: international meeting: discussion at U.S embassy',

4 July 1979, NAA A432 E1977/6390 Part 2.

53 G7 Tokyo Summit, *Special Statement of the Summit on Indochinese Refugees*, 28 June 1979.

54 R Woolcott, 'ASEAN Foreign Ministers' meeting – Indochinese refugees', 18 July 1979, NAA A432 E1977/6390 Part 2.

55 Submission no. 3327, Review of Indochinese Refugee Situation, July 1979, NAA A10756 LC1366 Part 2.

56 Submission no. 3327, Review of Indochinese Refugee Situation, July 1979.

57 'Double the intake', the *Canberra Times*, 2 July 1979, and 'Why we need more Vietnamese refugees', the *Australian Financial Review*, 21 June 1979, in Goodwin-Gill Collection.

58 UNHCR Office for Australia and New Zealand, *'Consultations on Indo-Chinese Refugees at the Headquarters in Geneva of the United Nations High Commissioner for Refugees on 11–12 December 1978'*, Press Release No. 25, 15 December 1978.

59 L Thomson, 'Indochinese refugees: Geneva meeting: second discussion at US embassy', 11 July 1979, NAA A432 E1977/6390 Part 2; Robinson, *Terms of Refuge*, 144.

60 'Indochinese Refugees – Minister's talks with Lord Carrington', 22 June 1979, NAA A432 E1977/6390 Part 2; HS Stokes, 'Japan to soften policy on refugees', the *New York Times*, 19 June 1979, 5.

61 Department of Foreign Affairs cable from Port Moresby to Canberra, 'Indochinese Refugees', 17 July 1979, NAA A432 E1977/6390 Part 2.

62 UNHCR, Submission to the Senate Legal and Constitutional Affairs References Committee Inquiry into the Incident at the Manus Island Detention Centre from 16 February to 18 February 2014, 7 May 2014, 7.

63 H Kamm, 'A confrontation on refugees', the *New York Times*, 28 June 1979, 4.

64 Wain, *The Refused*, 131.

65 Department of Foreign Affairs cable from Jakarta to Canberra, 'Indochinese Refugees', 20 June 1979, NAA A432 E1977/6390 Part 2.

66 Department of Foreign Affairs cable from Jakarta to Canberra, 'Indochinese Refugees', 20 June 1979.

67 UN General Assembly, *Meeting on Refugees and Displaced Persons in South-East Asia*.

68 Statement by Dr Guy Goodwin-Gill, Australian National University Conference on Indochinese Refugees, 30–31 July 1979; A Zolberg, A Suhrke and S Aguayo, *Escape from Violence: Conflict and the refugee crisis in the developing world*, Oxford University Press, New York, 1989, 166 f47.

69 R Koven, 'Vietnam vows to restrict departures of boat people', the *Washington Post*, 22 July 1979.

70 United Nations High Commissioner for Refugees, *The State of the World's Refugees: 2000 Fifty Years of Humanitarian Action*, UNHCR, Geneva, 2000, 79.

71   Zolberg, Suhrke and Aguayo, *Escape from Violence*, 167.
72   Australia. National Population Council, *Refugee Review*, Australian Government Publishing Service, Canberra, 79.
73   I Simington meeting with W Ismail, Kuala Lumpur, 13 November 1981, NAA A6980 S251347.
74   Submission no. 5439, 20 April 1982, NAA A12909 5439.
75   'Indochinese Refugees – direct arrival – Galang', 28 October 1983, NAA A1838 3020/10/4 Part 2.
76   I Macphee, Australia. *Commonwealth Parliamentary Debates*, House of Representatives, 1 May 1980, 2520.
77   I Macphee, Australia. *Commonwealth Parliamentary Debates*, House of Representatives, 1 May 1980, 2517–2518.
78   Interview with I Macphee, 8 December 2010; Smit, 'Malcolm Fraser's response to commercial refugee voyages', 91–94.
79   Macphee, Australia. *Commonwealth Parliamentary Debates*, House of Representatives, 1 May 1980, 2518.
80   I Macphee, Australia. *Commonwealth Parliamentary Debates*, House of Representatives, 20 October 1981, 2192–2194; J Menadue, *Things You Learn Along the Way*, David Lovell Publishing, Melbourne, 1999, 217; Interview with I Macphee, 8 December 2010.
81   Goodwin-Gill Collection, AUL: Reports, *UNHCR Sydney Branch Office, Report for December 1981*.
82   Goodwin-Gill Collection, AUL: Reports, *UNHCR Sydney Branch Office, Report for October 1981*.
83   Interview with I Macphee, 8 December 2010; Macphee, Australia. *Commonwealth Parliamentary Debates*, House of Representatives, 20 October 1981, 2192–2194.
84   C Brammall, 'Special pressure put on "illegals"', the *Canberra Times*, 30 January 1982, Goodwin-Gill Collection, DORS Gen.
85   Goodwin-Gill Collection, AUL: Reports, *UNHCR Sydney Branch Office, Report for 1981*.
86   'Deportation of illegal immigrants', *Commonwealth Record*, 27 December 1981, 1699.
87   Brammall, 'Special pressure put on "illegals"'.
88   Macphee, Australia. *Commonwealth Parliamentary Debates*, House of Representatives, 20 October 1981, 2194; Goodwin-Gill Collection, AUL: Reports, *UNHCR Sydney Branch Office, Report for 1981*.
89   Goodwin-Gill Collection, AUL: Reports, *UNHCR Sydney Branch Office, Report for 1981*.
90   Department of Immigration and Citizenship, *Submission to the Joint Select Committee on Australia's Immigration and Detention Network*, 20.
91   Interview with I Macphee, 8 December 2011, Melbourne (transcript with author).
92   Interview with I Macphee, 8 December 2011; Macphee, Australia.

Commonwealth Parliamentary Debates, House of Representatives, 20 October 1981, 2192–5.

93   I Macphee to M Fraser, 15 July 1981, NAA A1838 1634/75/1/3 Part 1.

94   I Macphee to M Fraser, 15 July 1981.

95   AC Helton, 'What is refugee protection?', in N Steiner, M Gibney and G Loescher, *Problems of Protection: The UNHCR, refugees and human rights*, Routledge, New York, 2003, 26.

96   Helton, 'What is refugee protection?', 23.

97   AC Helton, *The Price of Indifference: Refugees and humanitarian action in the new century*, Oxford University Press, Oxford, 2002, 253.

98   See further: S Taylor, 'Australia's "safe third country" provisions: Their impact on Australia's fulfilment of its *non-refoulement* obligations', *University of Tasmania Law Review*, 15(2), 1996, 196–235; A Schloenhardt, 'Australia and the boat people: Twenty-five years of unauthorised arrivals', *UNSW Law Journal*, 23(3), 2000, 48.

5   A relatively friendly affair

1   Goodwin-Gill Collection, DORS Gen, Note for File: concerning visit to Darwin 18–21 April 1979.

2   Goodwin-Gill Collection, DORS Gen, Note for File: concerning visit to Darwin 18–21 April 1979.

3   Goodwin-Gill Collection, DORS Gen, Note for File: concerning visit to Darwin 18–21 April 1979. See also: HV Le AO, Lieutenant Governor of South Australia, quoted in J Menadue, A Keski-Nummi and K Gauthier, *A New Approach: Breaking the stalemate on refugees and asylum seekers*, Centre for Policy Development, 2011, 17.

4   Goodwin-Gill Collection, DORS Gen, Note for File: concerning visit to Darwin 18–21 April 1979; See also: Interview with M MacKellar; Interview with D Volker.

5   Hoffmann, 40.

6   Goodwin-Gill Collection, DORS Gen, Note for File: concerning visit to Darwin 18–21 April 1979.

7   Goodwin-Gill Collection, DORS Gen, Note for File: concerning visit to Darwin 18–21 April 1979.

8   Goodwin-Gill Collection, DORS Gen, Note for File: concerning visit to Darwin 18–21 April 1979.

9   Goodwin-Gill Collection, DORS Gen, Note for File: concerning visit to Darwin 18–21 April 1979.

10   Goodwin-Gill Collection, DORS Gen, Note for File: concerning visit to Darwin 18–21 April 1979.

11   'Indochinese Refugees – Discussions in Washington 26–27 April 1978', NAA A6980 S251020 US–Australia refugee policy proposed – Washington visit – Part 3.

12   UN General Assembly, International Covenant on Civil and Political

Rights, 16 December 1966, 999 UNTS 171; UN General Assembly, Convention on the Rights of the Child, 20 November 1989, 1577 UNTS 3; Australian Human Rights Commission, *The Forgotten Children: national inquiry into children in Immigration detention*, Australian Human Rights Commission, Sydney, 2014, 11.

13   I Macphee, speech at the launch of P Mitchell, *Compassionate Bastard* (Penguin, Camberwell, 2011) at Glebe, NSW, 30 September 2011.

14   Interview with M Fraser.

15   Interview with M MacKellar.

16   Memorandum no. 380, Indochinese Refugees, 11 July 1979, NAA A12930 380.

17   L Engledow to M MacKellar, 'Boat refugees – alternative policy options'.

18   L Engledow to M MacKellar, 'Boat refugees – alternative policy options'.

19   L Engledow to M MacKellar, 'Boat refugees – alternative policy options'.

20   L Engledow to M MacKellar, 'Boat refugees – alternative policy options'.

21   L Engledow to M MacKellar, 28 April 1978.

22   D Volker, 'Indochinese Refugees – discussions in Washington 26–27 April 1978 – points of agreement'.

23   L Clinton Thompson, *Refugee Workers in the Indochina Exodus, 1975–1982*, McFarland & Co, Jefferson, 2010, 109–110.

24   D Volker, 'Indochinese Refugees – discussions in Washington 26–27 April 1978 – points of agreement'.

25   D Volker, 'Indochinese Refugees – discussions in Washington 26–27 April 1978 – points of agreement'.

26   Submission no. 2173 Indochinese Refugees – Programme for 1978/79, May 1978, NAA A10756 LC1366 – Part 1.

27   KS Hutchings, 'Notes on Cabinet Submission no. 2173 Indochinese Refugees – Programme for 1978/79', 4 May 1978, and 'Addendum to Submission no. 2173', 12 May 1978, NAA A10756 LC1366 – Part 1.

28   Decision no. 5258, 5 May 1978, and Decision no. 5372, 16 May 1978, NAA A10756 LC1366 – Part 1.

29   D Volker, 'Indochinese Refugees – Discussions in Washington 26–27 April 1978 – points of agreement'.

30   McAdam and Chong, 17–19.

31   KS Hutchings, 'Notes on Cabinet Submission no. 2173 Indochinese Refugees – Programme for 1978/79', 4 May 1978, and 'Addendum to Submission no. 2173', 12 May 1978, NAA A10756 LC1366 – Part 1.

32   KS Hutchings, 'Notes on Cabinet Submission no. 2173 Indochinese Refugees – Programme for 1978/79', 4 May 1978, and 'Addendum to Submission no. 2173', 12 May 1978.

33   'Payments and other arrangements for unauthorized arrivals', August 1979, NAA A1209 1979/1477 Part 1.

34   Submission no. 2572 Indochinese Refugees – report on visit to ASEAN capitals, August 1978, NAA A10756 LC1366 – Part 1.

35 L Engledow to M MacKellar, 'Boat refugees – alternative policy options'.

36 AC Kevin, 'Notes on Submission no. 2572, Indochinese Refugees – visit to ASEAN capitals', 7 September 1978, NAA A10756 LC1366 Part 1.

37 Submission no. 2771, 'Review of the Indochinese Refugee Program', NAA A10756 LC1366 Part 2.

38 L Engledow to M MacKellar, 13 November 1978, NAA A6980 S251099 Part 1.

39 M Mackellar, 'Speech to Austcare', *Commonwealth Record*, 26 November 1978, 1627.

40 Goodwin-Gill Collection, AUL: Reports, *UNHCR Sydney Branch Office, Report for January 1979*.

41 Submission no. 2771, 'Review of the Indo-Chinese refugee program', 17 November 1978, NAA A12909 2771.

42 AJ Ayers, 'Notes on cabinet submission 2771 review of the Indo-Chinese program', 24 November 1978, NAA A12909 2771.

43 'Refugee Boat *Hai Hong*', 8 November 1978, NAA A6980 S251099 Part 1.

44 Note to N Hoffmann, 8 November 1978, NAA A6980 S251099 Part 1; 'Christmas Island: call for refugee transit centre', the *Canberra Times*, 7 December 1978, 1.

45 P Everingham, Northern Territory of Australia. *Parliamentary Record*, Questions Without Notice, Legislative Assembly, 22 May 1979; Submission no. 3200, 25 May 1979, NAA 10756 LC1366 Part 2.

46 UN General Assembly, *Meeting on Refugees and Displaced Persons in South-East Asia*.

47 Submission no. 2771, 'Review of the Indo-Chinese refugee program', 17 November 1978, NAA A12909 2771.

48 R Holdich, 'Indochinese Refugees', 21 November 1978, NAA A10756 LC1366 Part 2.

49 Submission no. 2906, Review of Indochinese Refugee Situation, January 1979, NAA A12909 2906.

50 KS Hutchings, Notes on Cabinet Submission no. 2906, 19 January 1979, NAA A10756 LC1366 Part 2.

51 B Grant, *The Boat People: An 'Age' investigation with Bruce Grant*, Penguin Books, Melbourne, 1979, 205.

52 'Geneva Conference on Refugees – consultations between "like-minded" group and ASEAN officials', 19 July 1979, NAA A432 E1977/6390 Part 2.

53 'Geneva Conference on Refugees – consultations between "like-minded" group and ASEAN officials', 19 July 1979.

54 UN General Assembly, *Meeting on Refugees and Displaced Persons in South-East Asia*.

55 Submission no. 3169, May 1979, NAA A10756 LC1366 Part 2.

56 Submission no. 3169, May 1979.

57 Submission no. 3200: Legislation Against Unauthorised Boat Arrivals, 25 May 1979, NAA A10756 LC1366 Part 2; CD Samuel, Notes on

Cabinet Submission 3200: Legislation Against Unauthorised Boat Arrivals, 30 May 1979, NAA A10756 LC1366 Part 2.

58 Robinson, *Terms of Refuge*, 55, 194; L Hitchcox, *Vietnamese Refugees in Southeast Asian Camps*, Macmillan, London, 1990, 106–107.

59 Robinson, *Terms of Refuge*, 55. See also: A Missbach, 'Waiting on the islands of "stuckedness": Managing asylum seekers in island detention camps in Indonesia: from the late 1970s to early 2000s', *Austrian Journal of South-East Asian Studies (ASEAS)*, 6(2), 2013, 281–306.

60 CD Samuel, Notes on Cabinet Submission no. 3200: Legislation against unauthorized boat arrivals, 30 May 1979; M Ronai, Note for File: Treatment of unauthorized boat arrivals, 26 July 1979, NAA A1209 1979/1477 Part 1.

61 M Ronai, Note for File: Treatment of unauthorized boat arrivals.

62 B Juddery, 'Refugees and yet more refugees', the *Canberra Times*, 27 June 1979, 2.

63 CD Samuel, Notes on Cabinet Submission no. 3169, Processing Centre for Indo-Chinese Refugees, 11 May 1979, NAA A10756 LC1366 Part 2.

64 P Cornford, 'Camps may be only answer for refugees', the *Australian*, 21 June 1979.

65 MH Cass, Opposition Spokesman on Immigration and Ethnic Affairs, 'Indo-Chinese Boat People', Press Release, 24 April 1978.

66 'Labor lays down its policy: Temporary stay for boat people', the *Sydney Morning Herald*, 20 July 1979, in Goodwin-Gill Collection, DORS Gen.

67 'Labor lays down its policy: Temporary stay for boat people', the *Sydney Morning Herald*, 20 July 1979, in Goodwin-Gill Collection, DORS Gen.

68 'No transit camps', the *Sydney Morning Herald*, 20 July 1979, and 'No transit camps', the *Australian*, 20–21 July 1979, in Goodwin-Gill Collection, DORS Gen.

69 Editorial, 'No transit camps', the *Australian*.

70 S Milson, 'Wait and see policy on refugees', the *Sydney Morning Herald*, 20 July 1979, in Goodwin-Gill Collection, DORS Gen.

71 Milson, 'Wait and see policy on refugees'.

72 Milson, 'Wait and see policy on refugees'.

73 Decision no. 9149, Submission no. 3327 Review of Indo-Chinese Refugee Situation, 10 July 1979, NAA A12909 3327.

74 CD Samuel, 'Notes on Cabinet Submission no. 3327 Review of Indo-Chinese Refugee Situation', 9 July 1979, in NAA LC1366 Part 2.

75 Interview with M MacKellar.

76 Interview with M MacKellar.

77 Interview with M Fraser. See also: Fraser and Simons, *Malcolm Fraser: The political memoirs*, 419.

78 Interview with M MacKellar.

79 Interview with M MacKellar.

80 Fraser and Simons, *Malcolm Fraser: The political memoirs*, 419; Interview with M MacKellar.

81 Interview with M MacKellar.
82 Weller, *Malcolm Fraser PM*, 108. See also: P Weller, 'Prime Ministers and Cabinet', in P Weller (ed.), *Menzies to Keating: The development of the Australian prime ministership*, 16–17.
83 Interview with M MacKellar.
84 Fraser and Simons, *Malcolm Fraser: The political memoirs*, 420.
85 Interview with M Fraser. See also: Fraser and Simons, *Malcolm Fraser: The political memoirs*, 419.
86 Fraser and Simons, *Malcolm Fraser: The political memoirs*, 420.
87 M Steketee, 'Fraser rejected detention for boat people', the *Australian*, 1 January 2009.
88 Submission no. 3200 Legislation against unauthorised boat arrivals, May 1979, NAA A10122 D/52 Part 1 Cabinet Papers – Legislation against unauthorised boat arrivals.
89 'Report: Interdepartmental Committee on the Treatment of Unauthorised Boat Arrivals', NAA A446 1981/95004 Benefits for Unauthorised Boat Arrivals in Australia – Part 2.
90 See further: Goodwin-Gill Collection, DORS Gen, Note for File: concerning visit to Darwin 18–21 April 1979; R Vale to P Everingham, Northern Territory of Australia Parliamentary Record, Questions Without Notice, Legislative Assembly, 24 November 1977, 112; P Everingham, Northern Territory of Australia Parliamentary Record, *Debates*, Legislative Assembly, 11 May 1978, 1007–1008.
91 A Neaves to L Engledow, 25 October 1979, NAA A1209 1979/1477 Part 1.
92 A Neaves to L Engledow, 25 October 1979.
93 'Report: Interdepartmental Committee on the Treatment of Unauthorised Boat Arrivals', NAA A446 1981/95004 Benefits for Unauthorised Boat Arrivals in Australia – Part 2.
94 G Hand, Australia. *Commonwealth Parliamentary Debates*, House of Representatives, 5 May 1992, 2370.
95 Proceedings of the Conference on the Indochina Refugee Situation. See also: 'Australia not to have camps', the *Canberra Times*, 31 July 1979, 7.

6 Detention

1 Australia. Senate Standing Committee on Foreign Affairs and Defence, *Indochinese Refugee Resettlement: Australia's Involvement*, 825–839.
2 Australia. Senate Standing Committee on Foreign Affairs and Defence, *Indochinese Refugee Resettlement: Australia's Involvement*, 1171.
3 Goodwin-Gill Collection, AUL: Reports, *UNHCR Sydney Branch Office Report for 1981 to the United Nations High Commissioner for Refugees*; Goodwin-Gill Collection, AUL: Reports, *UNHCR Sydney Branch Office Report for 1982 to the United Nations High Commissioner for Refugees*.

4   Record of conversation between I Macphee and M Ghazali bin Shafie, Melbourne, 5 October 1981, NAA A1838 626/2/25 Part 1.

5   Australia. Department of Immigration and Ethnic Affairs, *Review of Activities to 30 June 1985*, Australian Government Publishing Service, Canberra, 64.

6   Australia. Department of Immigration and Ethnic Affairs, *Review of Activities to 30 June 1985*, 64.

7   See further: L Hardcastle and A Parkin, 'Immigration policy', in C Jennett and RG Stewart, *Hawke and Australian Public Policy: Consensus and restructuring*, MacMillan, Melbourne, 1990, 316–320.

8   F Bongiorno, *The Eighties: The decade that transformed Australia*, Black Inc., Melbourne, 2015, 64.

9   A Markus, *Race: John Howard and the remaking of Australia*, Allen & Unwin, Sydney, 2001, 63; L Carlyon, 'The racist tag doesn't worry me: Blainey', the *Sydney Morning Herald*, 1 May 1984, 1.

10   G Blainey, *All for Australia*, Methuen Haynes, Sydney, 1984, 13–14.

11   Blainey, *All for Australia*, 101–119.

12   P Kelly, *The End of Certainty: The story of the 1980s*, Allen & Unwin, Sydney, 1992, 34–36, 127–128; Markus, *Race*, 85.

13   M MacCallum, '"Mouth from the South" took Canberra by storm', the *Sydney Morning Herald*, 26 June 2013; Kelly, *The End of Certainty*, 128.

14   P Costigan, 'Stewart West stands firm in Asian storm', the *Herald*, 21 May 1984, 4.

15   A Buckley, 'Rage and tears as the House divides', the *Sydney Morning Herald*, 9 May 1984, 1.

16   Australia. *Commonwealth Parliamentary Debates*, House of Representatives, 8 May 1984, 1994–1997.

17   Buckley, 'Rage and tears as the House divides'.

18   A Peacock, in Australia. *Commonwealth Parliamentary Debates*, House of Representatives, 10 May 1984, 2232.

19   Interview with S West, 6 January 2012, Sydney (transcript with author).

20   Shadow Minister for Immigration and Ethnic Affairs, Michael Hodgman QC, *News Release*, 8 May 1984.

21   'Mr Peacock hits on race', the *Sydney Morning Herald*, 10 May 1984, 8.

22   'Migration: the counter-attack', the *Sydney Morning Herald*, 10 September 1984; 'Mr West answers his critics', the *Age*, 8 September 1984; 'Immigration policy reaffirmed', the *Sydney Morning Herald*, 31 May 1984.

23   Hardcastle and Parkin, 'Immigration policy', 320, 324.

24   Markus, *Race*, 59–67; A Markus, 'The politics of race', in D Gare, G Bolton, S Macintyre and T Stannage (eds), *The Fuss That Never Ended: The life and work of Geoffrey Blainey*, Melbourne University Press, Melbourne, 2003, 113.

25   Bongiorno, *The Eighties*, 83.

26   A Markus, J Jupp and P McDonald, *Australia's Immigration Revolution*, Allen
      & Unwin, Sydney, 2009, 91–92.
27   Interview with I Macphee, 8 December 2010; Interview with S West.
28   Interview with S West.
29   Jupp, *From White Australia to Woomera*, 128.
30   K Scott, 'Five Liberals break ranks', the *Canberra Times*, 26 August 1988, 1.
31   RJL Hawke, Australia. *Commonwealth Parliamentary Debates*, House of
      Representatives, 25 August 1988, 654–656.
32   Scott, 'Five Liberals break ranks'.
33   J Ryan, 'Why Ian Macphee crossed the floor of the house', the *Advertiser*, 7
      September 1988; Jupp, *From White Australia to Woomera*, 128.
34   Scott, 'Five Liberals break ranks'; Hardcastle and Parkin, 'Immigration
      policy', 325.
35   Markus, 'The politics of race', 113; Jupp, *From White Australia to Woomera*,
      46, 128; A Jukubowicz, 'We will fight them on the beaches ... :
      Australian immigration policy faces the new century', *Meanjin*, 3, 1999,
      107–108.
36   Bongiorno, *The Eighties*, 82–83.
37   Hage, 'Multiculturalism and White Paranoia in Australia', 429.
38   Bongiorno, *The Eighties*, 82–83.
39   R Hamlin, *Let Me Be a Refugee: Administrative justice and the politics of
      asylum in the United States, Canada, and Australia*, Oxford University Press,
      Oxford, 2014, 101–102.
40   Joint Standing Committee on Migration Regulations, *First Report – Illegal
      Entrants in Australia – Balancing Control and Compassion*, September 1990,
      Australian Government Publishing Service, Canberra, 37; M Crock, 'Judicial
      review and Part 8 of the Migration Act: necessary reform or overkill?', *Sydney
      Law Review*, 18, 1996, 275–280; M Crock, 'Judging refugees: The clash of
      power and institutions in the development of Australian refugee law', 54–57.
      See further: Hamlin, *Let Me Be a Refugee*, 110–111. See also: Australia.
      National Population Council, *Refugee Review*, 124.
41   Australia. Department of Immigration, Local Government and Ethnic
      Affairs, *Review 1990–91*, Australian Government Publishing Service,
      Canberra, 45. See further: *Chan v Minister for Immigration and Ethnic Affairs*
      (1989) 169 CLR 379.
42   Interview with W Gibbons.
43   M Crock, 'Apart from us or a part of us? Immigrants' rights, public opinion
      and the rule of law', *International Journal of Refugee Law*,
      10 (1998), 67, 72.
44   J Gao, *Chinese Activism of a Different Kind: The Chinese students' campaign
      to stay in Australia*, Brill, Leiden, 2013, 117, 155; Australia. Department
      of Immigration, Local Government and Ethnic Affairs, *Annual Report
      1991–92*, 82; G Chan, 'Cabinet papers 1988–89: Bob Hawke acted alone
      in offering asylum to Chinese students', the *Guardian*, 1 January 2015.

Extensions of this kind were not unusual, for example: extensions of
stay were granted in 1990 to Lebanese and Sri Lankans temporarily in
Australia, due to conditions within these countries of origin – Australia.
Department of Immigration, Local Government and Ethnic Affairs,
Annual Report 1990–91, 18.

45   J Jupp, *There Has to Be a Better Way: A long-term refugee strategy*, Australian
      Fabian Society, Arena Publications, Melbourne, 2003, 4; G Nicholls,
      'Unsettling admissions: Asylum seekers in Australia', *Journal of Refugee
      Studies*, 11(1), 1998, 63.

46   See further: Lawyers Committee for Human rights, *Seeking Shelter:
      Cambodians in Thailand, A report on human rights*, The Lawyers
      Committee for Human Rights, New York, 1987. See also: C Helton,
      'Asylum and refugee protection in Thailand', *International Journal of
      Refugee Law*, 1(1), 1989, 20–47.

47   S Erlanger, 'For Cambodians, joy and foreboding', the *New York Times*,
      24 September 1989; S Aitkin, 'Cambodians fear return to war', the
      Canberra Times, 18 September 1989, 6; KB Richburg, 'The hated Khmer
      Rouge fights on', the *Washington Post*, 22 October 1989; 'Khmer Rouge
      destroy government positions', the *Canberra Times*, 29 December 1989, 6.

48   'The voyage', undated circa December 1989, NAA A425 1989/4776.

49   'The voyage', and 'Maps, charts and traces', undated circa December 1989,
      NAA A425 1989/4776.

50   'Cambodian vessel – Pender Bay WA', 6 December 1989, NAA A425
      1989/4776, Coastwatch – Indo-Chinese Refugee Vessels.

51   Notated map, undated circa December 1989, NAA A425 1989/4776.

52   'Extracts from diary', undated circa December 1989, NAA A425
      1989/4776, Coastwatch – Indo-Chinese Refugee Vessels; C Amalfi,
      'Boat people's chart shows amazing 500km voyage', the *West Australian*,
      1 December 1989, 3.

53   'The voyage'.

54   'Summary and assessment', undated circa December 1989, NAA A425
      1989/4776.

55   Amalfi, 'Boat people's chart shows amazing 500km voyage'.

56   *A v Australia*, Communication No. 560/1993, UN Doc. CCPR/
      C/59/D/560/1993 (30 April 1997); J Phillips and H Spinks, *Immigration
      Detention in Australia*, Commonwealth Parliamentary Library, 20
      March 2013, <www.aph.gov.au/About_Parliament/Parliamentary_
      Departments/Parliamentary_Library/pubs/BN/2012-2013/Detention#_
      Toc351535439>, accessed 16 April 2017.

57   'Boat people sent to "bush camp"', the *Canberra Times*, 4 June 1990, 11.

58   Australia. Department of Immigration and Citizenship, *Submission to the
      Joint Select Committee on Australia's Immigration Detention Network*, 169.

59   Australia. Department of Immigration, Local Government and Ethnic
      Affairs, *Annual Report 1990–91*, 61.

60   Australia. Department of Immigration, Local Government and Ethnic
      Affairs, *Annual Report 1991–92*, 76.
61   Australia. Department of Immigration, Local Government and Ethnic
      Affairs, *Annual Report 1990–91*, 61.
62   See further: A Schloenhardt , 'Trafficking in Migrants: Illegal migration
      and organised crime in Australia and the Asia Pacific region', *International
      Journal of the Sociology of Law*, 29, 2001, 345–350, 369.
63   Australia. Department of Immigration, Local Government and Ethnic
      Affairs, *Annual Report 1990–91*, 63–64, 67; Australia. Department of
      Immigration, Local Government and Ethnic Affairs, *Annual Report
      1991–92*, 82.
64   Interview with W Gibbons.
65   G Campbell, Australia. *Commonwealth Parliamentary Debates*, House of
      Representatives, Grievance Debate, 8 October 1992, 1742.
66   I Simington, 'China, Hong Kong, immigration and Australia', in A
      Saikal (ed.), *Refugees in the Modern World*, Department of International
      Relations, Australian National University, Canberra, 1989, 97.
67   Simington, 'China, Hong Kong, immigration and Australia', 105.
68   N Blewett, *A Cabinet Diary: A personal record of the first Keating
      government*, Wakefield Press, Adelaide, 1999, 43.
69   B Birrell, 'The politics of the refugee issue', *People and Place*, 1(4), 1993, 9.
70   J McKiernan, 'The political imperative: Defend, deter, detain', in
      M Crock (ed.), *Protection or Punishment: The detention of asylum seekers in
      Australia*, Federation Press, Sydney, 1993, 4.
71   T Wright, 'PM's lone stand on refugees', the *Canberra Times*, 7 June 1990,
      1; P Mares, 'Australia's sledgehammer', Amnesty International, <apo.org.
      au/node/7240>, viewed 09 April 2017.
72   See further: *Mok v Minister of Immigration, Local Government and Ethnic
      Affairs* (1993) 47 FCR 1.
73   B Birrell, 'An interview with Mr Gerry Hand, former Minister for
      Immigration, Local Government and Ethnic Affairs', 6 October 1993,
      People and Place, 1(4), 6; T. Connors, 'Refugee damper needed: Evans',
      the *Canberra Times*, 16 June 1990, 3.
74   K Berry, *Cambodia: From red to blue: Australia's initiative for peace*, Allen
      & Unwin, Sydney, 1997, 20–21; Australia. *Commonwealth Parliamentary
      Debates*, Senate, 24 November 1989, 3298; K Scott, *Gareth Evans*,
      Allen & Unwin, Sydney, 1999, 263, 266–267. The peace settlement
      involved mass repatriation of more than 300 000 Cambodians from
      camps along the Thai border. See also: H Charlesworth, 'Kirby Lecture in
      International Law: Swimming to Cambodia: justice and ritual in human
      rights after conflict', *Australian Yearbook of International Law*, 29(1)
      2010, 1–16.
75   *A v Australia*; N. Poynder, 'A (Name Deleted) v Australia: a milestone for
      asylum seekers', *Australian Journal of Human Rights*, 4(1), 1997, 156.

76 G Robinson, 'Top-level mission to talk on boat-people', the *Canberra Times*, 7 June 1990, 2; 'Posted – on general duties?', the *Canberra Times*, 15 June 1990, 2.

77 Birrell, 'An interview with Mr Gerry Hand, former Minister for Immigration, Local Government and Ethnic Affairs', 2, 6.

78 P Mathew, 'Sovereignty and the right to seek asylum: The case of Cambodian asylum-seekers in Australia', *Australian Yearbook of International Law*, 35, 1994, 76.

79 Standing Committee on Refugees, Sub-Committee on Australia as a Country of First Asylum – Determination of Refugee Status, Second Meeting, Draft Report, 20 October 1977.

80 M Kingston, 'Boatpeople hardliner to leave Immigration', the *Canberra Times*, 9 June 1993, 3; M Kingston, 'Immigration raid after call by whistleblower', the *Canberra Times*, 30 April 1993, 3; *Mok v Minister of Immigration, Local Government and Ethnic Affairs* (1993) 47 FCR 1.

81 Birrell, 'An interview with Mr Gerry Hand, former Minister for Immigration, Local Government and Ethnic Affairs', 1–9.

82 Blewett, *A Cabinet Diary*, 16.

83 Blewett, *A Cabinet Diary*, 106.

84 See further: M Crock, 'Judging refugees: The clash of power and institutions in the development of Australian refugee law'; Mathew, 'Sovereignty and the right to seek Asylum: The case of Cambodian asylum-seekers in Australia', 35–101; S Taylor, 'How did we get here? A reflection on 25 years of Australian asylum seeker policy', *Law and Justice* blog, La Trobe Law School, 25 February 2016, <law.blogs.latrobe.edu.au/2016/02/25/how-did-we-get-here-a-reflection-on-25-years-of-australian-asylum-seeker-policy/>, accessed 16 April 2017. See also: Australia. Department of Immigration and Citizenship, *Submission to the Joint Select Committee on Australia's Immigration Detention Network*, September 2011, 173.

85 *A v Australia* [2.2-2.6].

86 Australia. Joint Standing Committee on Migration, *Asylum, Border Control and Detention*, Australian Government Publishing Service Canberra, 1994, 5.11.

87 Ministerial submission, 27 July 1985, NAA A1838 1690/1/6/3 Part 1. See also: K Neumann and S Taylor, 'Australia, Indonesia and West Papuan refugees, 1962–2009', *International Relations of the Asia–Pacific*, 10(1), 2010, 1–31.

88 Australia. Joint Standing Committee on Migration, *Asylum, Border Control and Detention*, 1994, 5.108.

89 Australia. Joint Standing Committee on Migration, *Asylum, Border Control and Detention*, 1994, 5.102.

90 *A v Australia* [7.13].

91 M Crock, 'Judicial review and part 8 of the *Migration Act*: Necessary reform or overkill?', *Sydney Law Review*, 283.

92   Blewett, *A Cabinet Diary*, 43, 106.
93   Blewett, *A Cabinet Diary*, 106.
94   K O'Brien, *Keating*, Allen & Unwin, Sydney, 2015, 758.
95   O'Brien, *Keating*, 461–462, 758.
96   See further: E Lester, *Making Migration Law: The foreigner, sovereignty and the case of Australia*, Cambridge University Press, Cambridge, 2017.
97   G Hand, Australia. *Commonwealth Parliamentary Debates*, House of Representatives, 5 May 1992, 2370.
98   M MacKellar, Australia. *Commonwealth Parliamentary Debates*, House of Representatives, 5 May 1992, 2383.
99   S Taylor, 'How did we get here?; K O'Brien, *Keating*, 758.
100   *Chu Kheng Lim v Minister for Immigration, Local Government and Ethnic Affairs* (1992) 176 CLR 1; Australia. Joint Standing Committee on Migration, *Asylum, Border Control and Detention*, 1994, 3.7–3.13. See also: J Chia, 'Back to the Constitution: The implications of *Plaintiff S4/2014* for immigration detention', *UNSW Law Journal*, 38(2), 2015, 633–652.
101   Australia. Department of Immigration and Ethnic Affairs, *Annual Report 1992–93*, 57; Department of Immigration and Citizenship, *Submission to the Joint Select Committee on Australia's Immigration Detention Network*, 170.
102   Australia. Joint Standing Committee on Migration, *Asylum, Border Control and Detention*, 1994, Table 2.10.
103   Australia. Department of Immigration and Ethnic Affairs, *Annual Report 1992–93*, 57; Mathew, 'Sovereignty and the right to seek asylum: The case of Cambodian asylum-seekers in Australia', 40.
104   Australia. Joint Standing Committee on Migration, *Asylum, Border Control and Detention*, 1994, 5.113; Mathew, 'Sovereignty and the right to seek asylum: The case of Cambodian asylum-seekers in Australia', 40, 101.
105   *A v Australia*, [9.4, 9.5].
106   Schloenhardt, 'Trafficking in migrants: Illegal migration and organised crime in Australia and the Asia Pacific region', 369.
107   A Carr, 'The engagement pendulum: Australia's alternating approach to irregular migration', *Journal of Australian Studies*, 40(3), 2016, 323–330.
108   R Bleiker, D Campbell, E Hutchinson and X Nicholson, 'The visual dehumanisation of refugees', *Australian Journal of Political Science*, 48(4), 2013, 412–413.
109   N Haslam and A Pedersen, *Yearning to breathe free: Seeking asylum in Australia*, The Federation Press, Sydney, 2007, 215.
110   F McKay, SL Thomas and S Kneebone, '"It would be okay if they came through the proper channels": Community perceptions and attitudes towards asylum seekers in Australia', *Journal of Refugee Studies*, 25(1), 2012, 114.
111   Australia. Department of Immigration and Citizenship, *Submission to the*

Joint Select Committee on Australia's Immigration and Detention Network, 19–20; UNHCR, *Asylum Applications Lodged in Industrialised Countries: 1980–1999*, Population Data Unit, Population and Geographic Data Section, Geneva, UNHCR, Nov. 2001, 52, <www.unhcr.org/3c3eb40f4. Pdf>, accessed 25 April 2017.

112 M Kingston, 'Politics and public opinion', in M Crock (ed.), *Protection or Punishment: The detention of asylum seekers in Australia*, 8–14.

113 PJ Keating, 'A time for reflection', Third Annual Manning Clark Lecture, Canberra, 3 March 2002, in PJ Keating, *Afterwords: The post-prime ministerial speeches*, Allen & Unwin, Sydney, 2011, 13.

How did we get here?

1 UN Human Rights Council, *Report of the Special Rapporteur on the human rights of migrants on his mission to Australia and the regional processing centres in Nauru*, 24 April 2017, A/HRC/35/25/Add.3, <www.refworld. org/docid/593a8c924.html>, accessed 18 June 2017.

2 Australia. Department of Foreign Affairs, *Annual Report 1980*, Australian Government Publishing Service, Canberra, 1981, 33.

3 Draft submission to Senate Standing Committee on Foreign Affairs and Defence inquiry, 1981, NAA A1838 932/32 Part 2.

4 See especially: Australian Human Rights Commission, *The Forgotten Children: national inquiry into children in Immigration detention*.

Index